40 Days

of

Prophetic

Miracles

40 Days

of

PROPHETIC

MIRACLES

DAVID KOMOLAFE

" . . . WILL PROPEL YOU INTO REVIVAL PRAYING AND
PRODUCE SIGNS AND WONDERS." - CHUCK. D. PIERCE.

WINEPRESS **WP** PUBLISHING

WinePress Publishing (PO Box 428, Enumclaw, WA 98022) functions only as book publisher. As such, the ultimate design, content, editorial accuracy, and views expressed or implied in this work are those of the author.

Unless otherwise indicated, all Scriptures is taken from the New King James Version. Copyright © 1982 by Thomas Nelson Inc. Used by permission. All rights reserved.

Scripture references marked kjv are taken from the King James Version of the Bible.

Scripture references marked niv are taken from the Holy Bible, New International Version, Copyright © 1973, 1978, 1984 by the International Bible Society. Used by permission of Zondervan Publishing House. The "NIV" and "New International Version" trademarks are registered in the United States Patent and Trademark Office by International Bible Society.

Scripture references marked nlt are taken from the Holy Bible, New Living Translation, copyright © 1996 by Tyndale Charitable Trust. Used by permission of Tyndale House Publishers, Wheaton, Illinois 60189. All rights reserved.

Scripture references marked nasb are taken from the New American Standard Bible, © 1960, 1963, 1968, 1971, 1972, 1973, 1975, 1977, 1995 by The Lockman Foundation. Used by permission.

ISBN 13: 978-1-57921-895-9
ISBN 10: 1-57921-895-4
Library of Congress Catalog Card Number: 2007920288
Printed in Colombia

ABOUT THE BOOK

This is a prayer book to propel you to a forty-day prophetic journey and make you step into the realm of miracles. It is more than a devotional book; rather it is to equip the weakest person for astounding supernatural experience.

It is a book born out of three decades of prophetic praying for the body of Christ. As a prophetic intercessor, I have seen God work unusual and uncommonly great things in prayer. I have been prophetically informed by the Spirit of the Almighty God of the revival of prayer and of signs and wonders as we approach the end of the age.

Where has the ministry of tears gone? The vehement, earnest, heartfelt prayers of the righteous produce wonderful miracles. "O Lord God! Set our hearts on fire for you again."

One of my roles in the Body of Christ is to develop prayer focuses that help God's people be disciplined in seeking Him, pressing through into a spiritual realm and experiencing His glorious blessings. Therefore, I am always looking for materials that can help equip the body of Christ *Forty Days of Prophetic Miracles* by Pastor David O. Komolafe is one of those self-help publications that will propel you into revival praying and produce signs and wonders. Pastor David explains the importance of forty day focus. Then he leads us step by step until we triumph and overcome past defeats, break into the Presence of God and break forth into miracles around us.

Chuck D. Pierce
President, Glory of Zion International Inc.
Vice President, Global Harvest Ministries
P. O. Box 1601
Denton, TX 76202

Forty Days of Prophetic Miracles is a practical how-to-book, born out of the author's experience. By following the instructions in this prayer book, your life will no longer remain the same. Break through miracles are guaranteed to become a reality in your life. Knowing how to pray will release your faith and will put you on the road to great victory and success.

Rev. Paul Browne Senior Pastor
Faith Alive International Ministries
Kingston, Ontario

Forty Days of Prophetic Miracles is a prophetic prayer to trouble the troublers and give rest to the troubled.

DEDICATION

This book is specially dedicated to every member of Above All Christian Gathering.

"He who comes from above is above all; . . . He who comes from heaven is above all."

(John 3:31)

TABLE *of* CONTENTS

ACKNOWLEDGEMENT

All the glory and adoration be unto the Lord Most High, the Holy One of Israel, who has set me apart from my mother's womb and called me by his grace to reveal Jesus to me. Thank God for Jesus who redeemed me by His blood and honor to the Holy Spirit my true Comforter.

I sincerely appreciate my divinely appointed helpmeet, Mercy, and my prophetic children, Esther, Grace and Shalom. They are blessings, indeed, to me. Thank God for the prophetic role of my mother, brothers, and sisters, they have been wonderfully supportive.

I am glad for the divine privilege to be the lead pastor of a loving, prayerful church—Above All Christian Gathering, Toronto, Canada. This is a wonderful, supportive congregation. God bless you all, in Jesus' name.

YOU MUST BE BORN AGAIN

"Do not marvel that I said to you, 'You must be born again.'"

(John 3:7)

One of life's greatest tragedies is to be lost and not realize it. Another tragedy is to be lost and know it, but not admit it or do anything about it. Life's greatest tragedy is to lose God and not to miss Him.

Man is helpless to save himself because "For all have sinned, and come short of the glory of God" (Romans 3:23). All are guilty before God. Sin came to the world by one man—Adam. When Adam sinned, sin entered the entire human race. Adam's sin brought death, so death spread to everyone, for everyone sinned. "For I was born a sinner—yes, from the moment my mother conceived me" (Psalm 51:5 NLT). "Your sins have cut you off from God . . ." (Isaiah 59:2, NLT). "For the Son of Man is come to seek and to save that which was lost" (Luke 19:10). Mankind is justified only by accepting God's plan of redemption. God has provided redemption by faith in Jesus Christ.

"That if you confess with your mouth, 'Jesus is Lord,' and believe in your heart that God has raised Him from the dead, you will be saved. For it is with your heart that you believe and are justified, and it is with your mouth that you confess and are saved" (Romans 10:9–10, NIV). "Repent, therefore, and be converted, that your sins may be blotted out, when the times of refreshing shall come from the presence of the Lord" (Acts 3:19).

- Acknowledge that you are lost and need a Savior— Jesus Christ.
- Confess your sins.
- Invite Him into your life as your Lord and Savior.
- Receive the grace of salvation and turn from your wicked ways.
- Thank God for the salvation of your soul
- Renounce every ungodly pursuit and habitually follow Jesus regardless of the price, not only when it is easy, convenient and popular. "Then He said to them all, 'If anyone desires to come after Me, let him deny himself, and take up his cross daily, and follow Me. For whoever desires to save his life will lose it, but whoever loses his life for My sake will save it. For what profit is it to a man if he gains the whole world, and is himself destroyed or lost? For whoever is ashamed of Me and My words, of him the Son of Man will be ashamed when He comes in His own glory, and in His Father's, and of the holy angels'" (Luke 9:23–26).

By making a decision to accept Jesus Christ as Lord and Savior, you escape eternal damnation unto eternal life. "For God so loved the world that He gave His only begotten Son, that whoever believes in Him should not perish but have everlasting life."

(John 3:16)

How to Use
This Book

You are about to start a Forty-day prophetic journey of miracles, glorious signs, and wonders. Each day will unfold abundant miracles in your life.

> "The end of a thing is better than its beginning; The patient in spirit is better than the proud in spirit."
> (Ecclesiastes 7:8)

However, your steps need divine guidance in this prophetic journey, so you will be established in miracles. This prayer book is divinely inspired to bring uncommon miracles and unforgettable blessings upon the body of Christ. I, therefore, encourage you to observe the following steps:

STEPS:

1. Be sure Jesus Christ reigns in you as Lord and Savior.
2. Get a prayer diary. Have a daily record of your personal encounters, visions, dreams, and revelations during these forty days of prophetic journey.
3. List your prayer requests—what you desire God to do for you—write them out.

4. At the end of the prayer section for each day, prayerfully present your request before God.
5. There is a prayer topic for each day of the forty days.
6. Most of the prayer topics are divided into four parts:
A. Praise and worship
B. It is written
C. Prophetic declarations
D. Prayer points

⊙ PRAISE AND WORSHIP
Spend quality time singing, praising, and worshiping God Almighty from the depth of your heart.

⊙ IT IS WRITTEN
When Jesus was tempted after forty days and forty nights of fasting and praying, on each occasion, He quoted the written word and "Then the devil left Him, and behold, angels came and ministered to Him" (Matthew 4:11). What is written is already written and established. Therefore, proclaim the written Word of God for it is powerful.

⊙ PROPHETIC DECLARATION:
This is an affirmation of your faith. Proclaim it loudly by faith.

⊙ PRAYER POINTS:
Jesus Christ, our supreme example, demonstrated the power of prayer for victorious living. Read what was written about His prayer life while on earth
"Who, in the days of His flesh, when He had offered up prayers and supplications, with vehement cries and tears to Him who was able to save Him from death, and was heard because of His godly fear, though He was a Son, yet

He learned obedience by the things which He suffered. And having been perfected, He became the author of eternal salvation to all who obey Him" (Hebrews 5:7–9).

Carefully read verse seven "When he had offered up prayers and supplications with vehement cries and tears . . ." In like manner, proceed on these forty days of prophetic miracle prayers with a holy and sincere cry unto God, who answers prayer. Speak it out.

Do not just read through, but say each point repeatedly. Do not lose focus and don't allow your mind to wander. Discipline your thoughts and be thankful in your heart.

7. Read carefully the introduction to each prayer topic before proceeding on the prayers.

8. "And they overcame him by the blood of the Lamb and by the word of their testimony, and they did not love their lives to the death" (Revelation 12:11). Be prepared to share your testimonies and be a true witness of God's wonder-working power.

9. Group prayer is a great blessing. Two or more people could gather each day in agreement for effectiveness. This book could also be used as a family devotional prayer book.

"Again I say to you that if two of you agree on earth concerning anything that they ask, it will be done for them by My Father in heaven. For where two or three are gathered together in My name, I am there in the midst of them" (Matthew 18:19–20).

10. Being alone with God is to encounter God's power. You can devote time on this prophetic journey as a personal spiritual revival. "Then Jacob was left alone; and a Man

wrestled with him until the breaking of day" (Genesis 32:24).

11. Schedule time each day and pray devotedly. When you start praying, be thorough with it. Do not interrupt the session.

INTRODUCTION

"Then you will call upon Me and go and pray to Me,
and I will listen to you. And you will seek Me and find
Me, when you search for Me with all your heart."
(Jeremiah 29:12–13)

This is the generation that has spoken much on prayer, published great books, organized prayer rallies and seminars with wonderful teachings on prayers, yet is allergic to praying.

Searching through history, no major revival has taken place without the earnest heartfelt, continued prayer of righteous men and women. Their prayers were dynamic, well-targeted, and full of power, thus producing wonderful results. I strongly perceive a revival of prophetic praying accompanied with signs and wonders as we approach the end of this age.

I will never forget an awesome divine encounter I had at a Scripture Union prayer meeting on September 15, 1975. The presence of God was so strong that the burden and the mantle of intercession rested on me. Since then, I have led several prayer groups and have seen God manifesting His greatness. My passion as a prophetic intercessor is to see God rebuilding the ancient ruins of prayer and restoring the joy of His presence to the body of Christ.

"You who hear prayer, to You all flesh will come."

(Psalm 65:2)

Why Forty Days?

1. Noah's flood. It rained upon the earth forty days and forty nights (Genesis 7:4, 12).
2. Moses was on the mount for forty days (Exodus 24:18).
3. Moses again, on the mount, fasting for forty days and forty nights (Exodus 34:28; Deuteronomy 9:9, 11, 18, 25; Deuteronomy 10:10).
4. The spies searched the Promised Land for forty days (Numbers 13:25).
5. Elijah fasted forty days and forty nights (I Kings 19:8).
6. Our Lord Jesus fasted for forty days and forty nights (Matthew 4:2).
7. Christ's post resurrection ministry was forty days (Acts 1:3).

Fasting may not be required, but you must have a sincere and repentant heart with faith toward God. I recommend partial or full-day fasting to sharpen your vision and revelations. For effective results, study the pages on "How to Use this Book" and ensure you have been redeemed by the blood of Jesus.

Through the prayers in this book, the lowliest and weakest person shall be equipped for greatness and miracles. These prayers shall trouble your "troublers" and give rest to the troubled. I encourage you to carefully pray through and never miss a day of praying.

My earnest prayer is that the anointing of the Holy Spirit will rest upon you for great signs and glorious wonders, in Jesus' name.

Day One
REPENTANCE

"Who may ascend into the hill of the LORD? Or who may stand in His holy place? He who has clean hands and a pure heart, who has not lifted up his soul to an idol, Nor sworn deceitfully. He shall receive blessing from the LORD, and righteousness from the God of his salvation."

(Psalm 24:3–5)

Making yourself right with God is the first step toward the manifestation of answered prayer. As you begin this forty-day journey, this first section of prayers restores your confidence and gives you boldness in approaching God's throne of grace and mercy.

Day One
REPENTANCE

PRAISE AND WORSHIP
IT IS WRITTEN

Who can understand his errors? Cleanse me from secret faults. Keep back Your servant also from presumptuous sins; Let them not have dominion over me. Then I shall be blameless, and I shall be innocent of great transgression" (Psalm 19:12–13).

"Do not remember the sins of my youth, nor my transgressions; according to Your mercy remember me, for Your goodness' sake, O LORD. For Your name's sake, O LORD, pardon my iniquity, for it is great" (Psalm 25:7, 11).

"Blessed is he whose transgression is forgiven, whose sin is covered. Blessed is the man to whom the LORD does not impute iniquity, and in whose spirit there is no deceit. I acknowledged my sin to You, and my iniquity I have not hidden. I said, I will confess my transgressions to the LORD, and You forgave the iniquity of my sin" (Psalm 32:1–2, 5).

"Wash me thoroughly from my iniquity, and cleanse me from my sin. For I acknowledge my transgressions, and my sin is always before me. Against You, You only, have I sinned, and done this evil in Your sight—that You may be found just when You speak, And blameless when You judge. Behold, I was brought forth in iniquity, and in sin my mother conceived me" (Psalm 51:2–5).

"If You, LORD, should mark iniquities, O Lord, who could stand? But there is forgiveness with You, that You may be feared" (Psalm 130:3–4).

"Search me, O God, and know my heart; try me, and know my anxieties; and see if there is any wicked way in me, and lead me in the way everlasting" (Psalm 139:23–24).

"O LORD, I know the way of man is not in himself; it is not in man who walks to direct his own steps. O LORD, correct me, but with justice; not in Your anger, lest You bring me to nothing" (Jeremiah 10:23–24).

"Turn us back to You, O LORD, and we will be restored; renew our days as of old" (Lamentations 5:21).

"And I prayed to the LORD my God, and made confession, and said, 'O LORD, great and awesome God, who keeps His covenant and mercy with those who love Him, and with those who keep His commandments, we have sinned and committed iniquity, we have done wickedly and rebelled, even by departing from Your precepts and Your judgments. To the Lord our God belong mercy and forgiveness, though we have rebelled against Him. O Lord, hear! O LORD, forgive! O LORD, listen and act! Do not delay for Your own sake, my God, for Your city and Your people are called by Your name'" (Daniel 9:4–5, 9, 19).

CONFESSION OF SIN

The LORD Most High, the High and Lofty One, who inhabits eternity, whose name is Holy, who dwells in the high and holy place (Isaiah 57:15), who humbles Himself to behold the things that are in heaven, and in the earth (Psalm 113:6).

"But we are all like an unclean thing, and all our righ-
teousnesses are like filthy rags; We all fade as a leaf, and
our iniquities, like the wind, have taken us away."

(Isaiah 64:6)

O LORD, according to all your righteousness, I beseech you,
let your anger and your fury be turned away from me, in Jesus'
name (Daniel 9:16).

According to your word, the eternal truth, "If we say
that we have no sin, we deceive ourselves, and the truth
is not in us. If we confess our sins, He is faithful and
just to forgive us our sins and to cleanse us from all
unrighteousness. If we say that we have not sinned, we
make Him a liar, and His word is not in us."

(1 John 1:8–10)

I humbly confess from the sincerity of my heart, that I have
sinned and fallen short of your glory (Romans 3:23).

"Who is a God like You, pardoning iniquity and pass-
ing over the transgression of the remnant of His heritage? He does not retain His anger forever, because He
delights in mercy. He will again have compassion on
us, and will subdue our iniquities. You will cast all our
sins into the depths of the sea."

(Micah 7:18–19)

"For the LORD will not cast off forever. Though He
causes grief, yet He will show compassion According to
the multitude of His mercies."

(Lamentations 3:31–32)

"The LORD is merciful and gracious, slow to anger, and abounding in mercy. He will not always strive with us, nor will He keep His anger forever. He has not dealt with us according to our sins, nor punished us according to our iniquities. For as the heavens are high above the earth, so great is His mercy toward those who fear Him; as far as the east is from the west, So far has He removed our transgressions from us. As a father pities his children, so the LORD pities those who fear Him. For He knows our frame; He remembers that we are dust."

(Psalm 103:8–14)

"Thanks be to God who has made Christ Jesus a sacrifice for my sin, who never sinned, but was made sin, so that I could be made right with God through Christ."

(2 Corinthians 5:21)

"For Christ also suffered once for sins, the just for the unjust, that He might bring us to God, being put to death in the flesh but made alive by the Spirit."

(1 Peter 3:18)

I, therefore, graciously receive forgiveness of my sin through the precious blood of the Lamb who was slain from before the foundation of the world.

O Lord God, pour your grace and mercy upon me that I may walk worthy and pleasing unto you, in Jesus' name.

Blood of Jesus, blot out the consequences of sin in my life, in Jesus' name.

Day Two

SELF-DELIVERANCE

With a humble heart and an act of faith, you can unseat thrones, dismantle strongholds, bind the strongman, and cast out all opposing forces. This prayer section breaks the legal hold of the enemy over your life. Do it believing and be fervent.

"I can do all things through Christ who strengthens me."

(Philippians 4:13)

Day Two
SELF-DELIVERANCE

PRAISE AND WORSHIP
IT IS WRITTEN

You have ascended on high, You have led captivity captive; You have received gifts among men, Even from the rebellious, That the LORD God might dwell there" (Psalm 68:18).

"When the LORD brought back the captivity of Zion, we were like those who dream. Then our mouth was filled with laughter, and our tongue with singing. Then they said among the nations, 'The LORD has done great things for them.' The LORD has done great things for us, and we are glad. Bring back our captivity, O LORD, as the streams in the South" (Psalm 126:1–4).

"Awake, awake! Put on your strength, O Zion; put on your beautiful garments, O Jerusalem, the holy city! For the uncircumcised and the unclean shall no longer come to you. Shake yourself from the dust, arise; sit down, O Jerusalem! Loose yourself from the bonds of your neck, O captive daughter of Zion! For thus says the LORD: 'You have sold yourselves for nothing, and you shall be redeemed without money'" (Isaiah 52:1–3).

"'For behold, I have made you this day a fortified city and an iron pillar, and bronze walls against the whole land—against the kings of Judah, against its princes, against its priests, and against the people of the land. They will fight against you, but they shall not prevail against you. For I am with you,' says the LORD, 'to deliver you'" (Jeremiah 1:18–19).

"Therefore God also has highly exalted Him and given Him the name which is above every name, that at the name of Jesus every knee should bow, of those in heaven, and of those on earth, and of those under the earth" (Philippians 2:9–11).

"Giving thanks to the Father who has qualified us to be partakers of the inheritance of the saints in the light. He has delivered us from the power of darkness and conveyed us into the kingdom of the Son of His love, in whom we have redemption through His blood, the forgiveness of sins" (Colossians 1:12–14).

"But you are a chosen generation, a royal priesthood, a holy nation, His own special people, that you may proclaim the praises of Him who called you out of darkness into His marvelous light; who once were not a people but are now the people of God, who had not obtained mercy but now have obtained mercy" (1 Peter 2:9–10).

"For whatever is born of God overcomes the world. And this is the victory that has overcome the world—our faith" (1 John 5:4).

"He who leads into captivity shall go into captivity; he who kills with the sword must be killed with the sword. Here is the patience and the faith of the saints" (Revelation 13:10).

PROPHETIC DECLARATION

"For it is God who works in you both to will and to do for His good pleasure" (Philippians 2:13).

I shall surely fulfill the good pleasure of my Lord and Savior Jesus Christ. I am a citizen of heaven, and I am seated together with Christ Jesus in heavenly realms. I refuse to be intimidated by my adversaries because my Lord Jesus Christ has made me free—I am really and unquestionably free.

"You are my hiding place; You shall preserve me from trouble; You shall surround me with songs of deliverance" (Psalm 32:7).

PRAYER POINTS:

1. Prayerfully carry out these steps on each of the under-listed items:

   Step One: Repentance.
   Step Two: Bind the powers involved in Jesus name.
   Step Three: Break the covenant in the name of Jesus.
   Step Four: Command to depart and never return in Jesus' name.
   Step Five: Ask the blood of Jesus to nullify the evil consequences.
   Step Six: Seal up the door it has opened by the blood of Jesus.
   Step Seven: Command no re-enforcement in Jesus' name.
   Step Eight: Command all the good things it has hindered to manifest now in Jesus' name.
   Step Nine: Ask the Holy Spirit to fill the space that was occupied in Jesus' name.

−	Spirit of Fear	−	Spirit of Error
−	Spirit of Rejection	−	Spirit of Pride
−	Spirit of Heaviness	−	Spirit of Frustration
−	Spirit of Depression	−	Spirit of Irritation
−	Spirit of Aimlessness	−	Spirit of Vanity

−	Spirit of Calamity	−	Spirit of Doubt
−	Spirit of Defeat		Spirit of Slumber
−	Spirit of Failure	−	Serpentine spirit
−	Spirit of Discouragement	−	Witchcraft spirit
−	Spirit of Suicide	−	Familiar spirit
−	Spirit of Accident-proneness	−	Spirit of Rebellion
−	Spirit of Condemnation	−	Spirit of Seduction
−	Spirit of Addiction	−	Spirit of Treachery
−	Spirit of Gluttony	−	Spirit of Bitterness

2. Whatever is resisting the deliverance of the LORD in my life, be destroyed by the blood of Jesus.
3. I fire arrows of deliverance into the foundation of my life, in Jesus' name (2 Kings 13:17).
4. Holy Spirit, fill me unto overflowing in Jesus' name.
5. Thank God for answered prayers in Jesus' name.

Day Three
REPAIRING THE FOUNDATION

"If the foundations are destroyed, what can the righteous do?"

(Psalm 11:3)

You must repair the foundation to have a long-lasting blessing; work on your foundation. The foundation is the root of your life that anchors your destiny. The quality of your life and how well established you are in the good things of life, will be determined by your foundation. Allow the purging fire of the Holy Spirit to repair your foundation.

Day Three

REPAIRING THE
FOUNDATION

PRAISE AND WORSHIP
IT IS WRITTEN

For their rock is not like our Rock. Even our enemies themselves being judges" (Deuteronomy 32:31).

"Of old You laid the foundation of the earth, and the heavens are the work of Your hands" (Psalm 102:25).

"When the whirlwind passes by, the wicked is no more, but the righteous has an everlasting foundation" (Proverbs 10:25).

"Therefore thus says the LORD God: Behold, I lay in Zion a stone for a foundation, A tried stone, a precious cornerstone, a sure foundation; Whoever believes will not act hastily" (Isaiah 28:16).

"And even now the ax is laid to the root of the tree. Therefore every tree which does not bear good fruit is cut down and thrown into the fire" (Matthew 3:10).

"But He answered and said, 'Every plant which My heavenly Father has not planted will be uprooted'" (Matthew 15:13).

"And I also say to you that you are Peter, and on this rock I will build My church, and the gates of Hades shall not prevail against it. And I will give you the keys of the kingdom of heaven, and whatever you bind on earth will be bound in heaven, and whatever you loose on earth will be loosed in heaven" (Matthew 16:18 19).

"For no other foundation can anyone lay than that which is laid, which is Jesus Christ" (1 Corinthians 3:11).

"Nevertheless the solid foundation of God stands, having this seal: 'The Lord knows those who are His,' and, 'Let everyone who names the name of Christ depart from iniquity'" (2 Timothy 2:19).

PROPHETIC DECLARATION

Jesus Christ is my sure foundation, my Rock of refuge and my Deliverer, arise and defend Your interest in my life. My Lord Jesus, rescue my foundation from corruption and destruction. "He will sit as a refiner and a purifier of silver; He will purify the sons of Levi, And purge them as gold and silver, that they may offer to the LORD an offering in righteousness" (Malachi 3:3).

PRAYER POINTS

1. It is written: "If the foundations are destroyed, what can the righteous do?" (Psalm 11:3). Therefore Jehovah my Mighty Creator; deliver my foundation from destruction, in Jesus' name.

2. It is written: "For our God is a consuming fire" (Hebrews 12:29). Therefore, consuming fire of my living God, flush captivity out of my life in Jesus' name.

3. In the name of Jesus, I command darkness to depart from my foundation.

4. It is written: "Then God said, 'Let there be light'; and there was light" (Genesis 1:3). Therefore, Light of the Almighty God; appear in my foundation in Jesus' name.

5. It is written: ". . . and the firmament shows his handiwork" (Psalm 19:1). Therefore, O firmament, proclaim God's greatness in my life, in Jesus' name.

6. It is written: "Let the skies pour down righteous" (Isaiah 45:8). Therefore, pour down on me the blessing you hold in the sky in Jesus' name.

7. It is written: "Let the earth open and let them bring forth salvation, and let righteousness spring up together; I the Lord, have created it" (Isaiah 45:8). Therefore, O earth, give up my hidden treasure unto me now, in Jesus' name.

8. It is written: "And God said, 'Let the waters bring forth abundantly'" (Genesis 1:20). Therefore, let my blessings in the body of water come forth now, in Jesus' name.

9. It is written: "You divided the sea by Your strength; You broke the heads of the sea serpents in the waters. You broke the heads of Leviathan in pieces, and gave him as food to the people inhabiting the wilderness" (Psalm 74:13–14). Therefore, O arm of God, shatter asunder the leviathan attack against my life, in Jesus' name.

10. It is written: "He raises the poor out of the dust, and lifts the needy out of the ash heap" (Psalm 113:7). Therefore, in the name of Jesus, I break free and break loose from the power of the dung.

11. You, power of the dust, you shall not waste my destiny, in Jesus' name.

12. O Lord God, raise me up and lift me from the pit, in Jesus' name.

13. In the name of Jesus I command evil yokes and evil burdens to depart from my life.

14. Blood of Jesus, repair the foundation of my destiny, in Jesus' name.

15. My Lord Jesus, be enthroned in my foundation, in Jesus' name.

16. Holy Spirit, unfold the secret of greatness and success in my life, in Jesus' name.

17. It is written: "That He may seat him with princes—with the princes of His people" (Psalm 113:8). Therefore, O Lord God, set me with the princes of the land and exalt me with favor, in Jesus' name.

18. It is written: "You will arise and have mercy on Zion; For the time to favor her, yes, the set time, has come" (Psalm 102:13). Therefore, hasten to fulfill this written word in my life, O God, in Jesus' name.

19. O Lord God, cause the arrogance of the proud to cease in my life, in Jesus' name (Isaiah 13:11).

20. O Lord God, lay low the haughtiness of the terrible in my life, in Jesus' name (Isaiah 13:11).

21. It is written: "It shall come to pass in the day the LORD gives you rest from your sorrow and from your fear and the hard bondage in which you were made to serve" (Isaiah 14:3). Therefore, O Lord God, give me rest from sorrow, fear, and from hard bondage, in Jesus' name.

22. My foundational glory, be restored now, in Jesus' name.

23. Holy Spirit, fortify my foundation for mighty miracles, in Jesus' name.

24. Give thanks to God for answered prayer, in Jesus' name.

Day Four
VICTORY THROUGH THE BLOOD

"Nothing but the blood of Jesus," says the song writer. Absolutely nothing in heaven, on earth and under the earth can resist the efficacious blood of Jesus. If used as a spiritual weapon, it avails wonderfully.

"And according to the law almost all things are purified with blood, and without shedding of blood there is no remission."

(Hebrews 9:22)

Day Four

Victory Through the Blood

PRAISE AND WORSHIP
IT IS WRITTEN

Now the blood shall be a sign for you on the houses where you are. And when I see the blood, I will pass over you; and the plague shall not be on you to destroy you when I strike the land of Egypt" (Exodus 12:13).

"For the life of the flesh is in the blood, and I have given it to you upon the altar to make atonement for your souls; for it is the blood that makes atonement for the soul" (Lev. 17:11).

"Much more then, having now been justified by His blood, we shall be saved from wrath through Him" (Romans 5:9).

"In Him we have redemption through His blood, the forgiveness of sins, according to the riches of His grace" (Ephesians 1:7).

"By so much more Jesus has become a surety of a better covenant" (Hebrews 7:22).

"And according to the law almost all things are purified with blood, and without shedding of blood there is no remission" (Hebrews 9:22).

"But if we walk in the light as He is in the light, we have fellowship with one another, and the blood of Jesus Christ His Son cleanses us from all sin" (1 John 1:7).

LET THE BLOOD SPEAK

I am in a covenant relationship with the blood of Jesus.

The blood of Jesus gives me victory in battle, healing in sickness, success in life, power over stubborn pursuers and makes me strong in the Lord and in the power of His might.

The blood of Jesus is undefiled, unpolluted and the perfect ransom for my soul. The blood of Jesus is my eternal mark of distinction, which grants me entrance into the court of heaven and a guarantee of better living.

It is written: "And they overcame Him by the Blood of the Lamb and by the word of their testimony" (Revelation 12:11). These are words of my testimonies:

- Through the blood of Jesus, I have been redeemed out of the hands of the evil ones.
- The blood of Jesus cleanses me from all sins.
- Through the blood of Jesus, I am justified, sanctified and made holy.
- Through the blood of Jesus, I have the life of God in me.
- Through the blood of Jesus, I have access to the presence of God, and I enter into the Holy of Holies by the blood of Jesus.

I, therefore, sprinkle the blood of Jesus upon myself and my household.

I sprinkle the blood of Jesus on my environment. I hold the blood of Jesus as a shield against any power, spirit or personality resisting the glory of God in my life.

I hold the blood of Jesus against sicknesses and diseases in my life, because it is written: "And the LORD will take away from you all sickness, and will afflict you with none of the terrible diseases of Egypt which you have known, but will lay them on all those who hate you" (Deuteronomy 7:15).

I hold the blood of Jesus against evil prophecies and visions set against my life, because it is written: "Let not a slanderer be established in the earth; Let evil hunt the violent man to overthrow him" (Psalm 140:11).

Therefore, every evil prophesy and vision against my life be abolished by the blood of Jesus.

I hold the blood of Jesus against every evil thought and imagination set against my life because it is written: "Do not grant, O LORD, the desires of the wicked; Do not further his wicked scheme, lest they be exalted" (Psalm 140:8).

I declare every evil expectation for my life to be nullified by the blood of Jesus. "And to the blood of sprinkling that speaks better things than that of Abel" (Hebrews 12:24). Therefore, Thou voice of the blood of Jesus speak victory into my life, in Jesus' name.

Thou precious blood of Jesus, minister defeat to every evil work in my life, in Jesus' name.

It is written: "Having wiped out the handwriting of requirements that was against us, which was contrary to us. And He has taken it out of the way, having nailed it to the cross" (Colossians 2:14).

Therefore, every evil mark upon my life be blotted out by the blood of Jesus.

Day Five

OVERCOMING FEAR

Fear is a weapon of torment, torture and captivity. So many people are fearful of war, enemies, death, evil, ghost, darkness, future, even men. The worst of all is imaginative fear, fear of nothing; this is killing.

Fear gives the adversary of your soul courage to attack you. Therefore, when you honor God with your life, reverence and respect Him enough, it dispels your fear.

I trust the Holy Spirit to strengthen your inner-man as you pray to overcome fear, in Jesus' name.

"Have I not commanded you? Be strong and of good courage; do not be afraid, nor be dismayed, for the LORD your God is with you wherever you go."

(Joshua 1:9)

Day Five
OVERCOMING FEAR

PRAISE AND WORSHIP
IT IS WRITTEN

So he answered, 'Do not fear, for those who are with us are more than those who are with them'" (2 Kings 6:16).

"The LORD is my light and my salvation; whom shall I fear? the LORD is the strength of my life; of whom shall I be afraid? When the wicked came against me to eat up my flesh, my enemies and foes, they stumbled and fell. Though an army may encamp against me, my heart shall not fear; though war may rise against me, in this I will be confident" (Psalm 27:1–3).

"Do not be afraid of sudden terror, nor of trouble from the wicked when it comes; for the LORD will be your confidence, and will keep your foot from being caught" (Proverbs 3:25–26).

"For you did not receive the spirit of bondage again to fear, but you received the Spirit of adoption by whom we cry out, 'Abba, Father'" (Romans 8:15).

"For though we walk in the flesh, we do not war according to the flesh. For the weapons of our warfare are not carnal but mighty in God for pulling down strongholds, casting down arguments and every high thing that exalts itself against the knowledge of God, bringing every thought into captivity to the obedience of Christ, and being ready to punish all disobedience when your obedience is fulfilled" (2 Corinthians 10:3–6).

"For God has not given us a spirit of fear, but of power and of love and of a sound mind" (2 Timothy 1:7).

"And release those who through fear of death were all their lifetime subject to bondage" (Hebrews 2:15).

"So we may boldly say: 'The Lord is my helper; I will not fear. What can man do to me?'" (Hebrews 13:6).

"There is no fear in love; but perfect love casts out fear, because fear involves torment. But he who fears has not been made perfect in love" (1 John 4:18).

PROPHETIC DECLARATION:

I enthrone Jesus Christ in my life. I reverence and honor God Almighty, my heavenly Father, and I put my entire trust in Him. My heart is established in Christ; therefore, I am not afraid of death because Christ Jesus has given me life, even abundant life. I am not afraid of danger, neither am I afraid of enemies nor the wicked because, "greater is He that is in me, than he that is in the world" (1 John 4:4). My future is secured in Christ Jesus because; "I'm more than a conqueror through Christ that loved me" (Romans 8:37). "If God be for me, who can be against me" (Romans 8:31). Therefore, I overcome fear, panic attacks and emotional disorder by the blood of the Lamb, Jesus Christ and by this declaration, in Jesus' name.

PRAYER POINTS

1. In the name of Jesus, I reject and bind the spirit of fear.
2. In the name of Jesus, I break covenant with fear.
3. In the name of Jesus, I cast down the stronghold of fear in my life.

4. Every inherited fear controlling the affairs of my life, loosen your hold and flee, in Jesus' name.

5. It is written: "For the thing which I greatly feared is come upon me, and that which I was afraid of is come unto me" (Job 3:25, KJV). Therefore, I declare that the things which I greatly feared will not come upon me and that which I am afraid of shall not come upon me, in Jesus' name.

6. Every arrow of fear fired at me, loosen your hold and flee, in Jesus' name.

7. In the name of Jesus, I break loose from the captivity of fear.

8. Every danger signal set at me, be nullified by the blood of Jesus.

9. Torment of fear, release me now, in Jesus' name.

10. The networking of internal and external fear in my life, break asunder, in Jesus' name.

11. I decree to my heart, be established in Lord Jesus and be fortified in the Holy Spirit, in Jesus' name.

12. It is written: "The righteous are bold as a lion" (Proverbs 28:1). Therefore, I decree boldness of the Holy Spirit into my life, in Jesus' name.

13. Holy Spirit fire, drain fear out of my life, in Jesus' name.

14. Every good thing that fear has taken from me be restored unto me now in Jesus' name.

15. My Lord Jesus, strengthen my faith in You, in Jesus' name.

16. I shall not suffer shipwreck of my faith, in Jesus' name.

17. I proclaim before the Lord God Almighty that my confident trust in Him shall not fail, in Jesus' name.

18. I refuse to yield to evil commands, in Jesus' name.

19. The voice of oppression over my life be silenced, in Jesus' name.
20. In Jesus' name, I step out of the bondage of fear.
21. The fear of future of my life, turn to success, in Jesus' name.
22. Joy and peace in the Holy Spirit, overwhelm my soul, in Jesus' name.
23. The never-failing undefeated champion in me, manifest now, in Jesus' name.
24. Give thanks to God for answered prayers.

Day Six
OPEN HEAVEN

"And your heavens which are over your head shall be bronze, and the earth which is under you shall be iron."

(Deuteronomy 28:23)

Operating under a closed heaven makes life extremely difficult, harsh, and bitter. Therefore, for continuous flow of God's power and presence, your heavens must be opened. In this prophetic journey to miracles, ensure that your heaven is open for the continuous outpouring of God's glory. This prayer section is well targeted to unlock the flood gates of heaven for the manifestation of God's goodness in your life.

Day Six
OPEN HEAVEN

PRAISE AND WORSHIP
IT IS WRITTEN

Then he dreamed, and behold, a ladder was set up on the earth, and its top reached to heaven; and there the angels of God were ascending and descending on it. And behold, the LORD stood above it and said: 'I am the LORD God of Abraham your father and the God of Isaac; the land on which you lie I will give to you and your descendants. Also your descendants shall be as the dust of the earth; you shall spread abroad to the west and the east, to the north and the south; and in you and in your seed all the families of the earth shall be blessed. Behold, I am with you and will keep you wherever you go, and will bring you back to this land; for I will not leave you until I have done what I have spoken to you.' . . . And he was afraid and said, 'How awesome is this place! This is none other than the house of God, and this is the gate of heaven!'" (Genesis 28:12–15, 17).

"And the angel of the LORD appeared to him in a flame of fire from the midst of a bush. So he looked, and behold, the bush was burning with fire, but the bush was not consumed" (Exodus 3:2).

"And it happened, as they fled before Israel and were on the descent of Beth Horon, that the LORD cast down large hailstones from heaven on them as far as Azekah, and they died. There were more who died from the hailstones than the children of Israel killed with the sword" (Joshua 10:11).

"They fought from the heavens; the stars from their courses fought against Sisera" (Judges 5:20).

"Rain down, you heavens, from above, And let the skies pour down righteousness; Let the earth open, let them bring forth salvation, and let righteousness spring up together. I, the LORD, have created it" (Isaiah 45:8).

"It shall come to pass in that day that I will answer," says the LORD; "I will answer the heavens, and they shall answer the earth. The earth shall answer with grain, with new wine, and with oil; They shall answer Jezreel" (Hosea 2:21–22).

"For thus says the LORD of hosts: 'Once more (it is a little while) I will shake heaven and earth, the sea and dry land'" (Hag. 2:6).

"When He had been baptized, Jesus came up immediately from the water; and behold, the heavens were opened to Him, and He saw the Spirit of God descending like a dove and alighting upon Him. And suddenly a voice came from heaven, saying, 'This is My beloved Son, in whom I am well pleased'" (Matthew 3:16–17).

"After these things I looked, and behold, a door standing open in heaven. And the first voice which I heard was like a trumpet speaking with me, saying, 'Come up here, and I will show you things which must take place after this'" (Revelation 4:1).

PROPHETIC DECLARATION

"Oh, that You would rend the heavens! That You would come down! That the mountains might shake at Your presence—as fire burns brushwood, as fire causes water to boil—to make

Your name known to Your adversaries, that the nations may tremble at Your presence! When You did awesome things for which we did not look, You came down; the mountains shook at Your presence. For since the beginning of the world men have not heard nor perceived by the ear, nor has the eye seen any God besides You, who acts for the one who waits for Him" (Isaiah 64:1–4). Therefore, O Lord God of heaven, open up your heaven and hear me. Flood gates of heaven, open unto me, in Jesus' name.

PRAYER POINTS

1. Any iniquity that has closed heaven against me be blotted out by the blood of Jesus, in Jesus' name.
2. O ye principalities inhabiting my heaven, be shattered asunder, in Jesus' name.
3. Evil trafficking in my heavens, scatter to desolations, in Jesus' name.
4. Evil strongholds and altars, in the heavenlies against me, fire from heaven consume them, in Jesus' name.
5. It is written: "The sun shall not strike you by day, nor the moon by night" (Psalm 121:6). Therefore, the sun, the moon and the stars shall not bewitch my life, in Jesus' name.
6. Every evil projection into the sun, the moon and the stars against my life, be abolished by the blood of Jesus.
7. Summoning by the sun, the moon and the stars against my life, perish, in Jesus' name.
8. It is written: "You are wearied in the multitude of your counsels; Let now the astrologers, the stargazers, and the monthly prognosticators Stand up and save you from what shall come upon you. Behold, they shall be as stubble, the fire shall burn them; they shall not deliver themselves from the power of the flame; it shall

not be a coal to be warmed by, nor a fire to sit before!" (Isaiah 47:13 14). Therefore, fire from heaven, con sume the astrologers, star gazers and prognosticators, set against my life, in Jesus' name.

9. Spirit of disorderliness shall not prevail in my life, in Jesus' name.

10. O Lord God of Host ride swiftly upon the heaven to my help, in Jesus' name.

11. It is written: "For he hath broken the gates of brass, and cut the bars of iron in sunder" (Psalm 107:16, KJV). Therefore, gates of brass and bars of iron over my heavens, in the name of Jesus, be shattered asunder.

12. In the name of Jesus, the heavens over my life shall not be closed.

13. O gates of heaven and earth, un-cage my glory, in Jesus' name.

14. I enthrone the Lordship of Jesus over my heavens, in Jesus' name.

15. War in the heavenly places against my life; be subdued by the blood of Jesus, in Jesus' name.

16. O heaven of heavens, pour your glory upon my life, in Jesus' name.

17. It is written: "The heavens were opened, and I saw visions of God" (Ezekiel 1:1). Therefore, O visions of God, ignite my life in Jesus' name.

18. My spirit man, connect to your divine position, in Jesus' name.

19. My blessings due to me in heavenly places, pour on me now, in Jesus' name.

20. My due season of blessings has come, O heaven, rain on me, in Jesus' name.

21. O heaven, open unto me your good treasure, in Jesus' name.

22. O blood of Jesus, anoint me for greatness, in Jesus'
    name.
23. Henceforth, I shall abound in open heaven, in Jesus'
    name.
24. Give thanks to God for answered prayers.

Day Seven
TERRITORIAL DOMINION

"For the earnest expectation of the creation eagerly waits for the revealing of the sons of God."

(Romans 8:19)

Until you arise in authority to take your environment for the kingdom of God, and of His Son, Jesus Christ, the evil around you may keep re-enforcing its wickedness. It's time to establish your dominion in Christ in all areas of your life. March forward triumphantly; never lose focus for victory is certain.

Day Seven
TERRITORIAL DOMINION

PRAISE AND WORSHIP
IT IS WRITTEN

I n the beginning God created the heavens and the earth"
(Genesis 1:1).

"The earth is the LORD's, and all its fullness, the world and
those who dwell therein. For He has founded it upon the seas,
and established it upon the waters" (Psalm 24:1–2).

"He makes wars cease to the end of the earth; he breaks the
bow and cuts the spear in two; he burns the chariot in the fire.
Be still, and know that I am God; I will be exalted among the
nations, I will be exalted in the earth! The LORD of hosts is
with us; the God of Jacob is our refuge" (Psalm 46:9–11).

"Behold, the nations are as a drop in a bucket, and are counted as the small dust on the scales; look, He lifts up the isles as
a very little thing. . . . All nations before Him are as nothing,
and they are counted by Him less than nothing and worthless"
(Isaiah 40:15, 17).

"It is He who sits above the circle of the earth, and its inhabitants are like grasshoppers. He stretches out the heavens like a
curtain, and spreads them out like a tent to dwell in. He brings

the princes to nothing; he makes the judges of the earth useless" (Isaiah 40:22–23).

"Do not remember the former things, nor consider the things of old. Behold, I will do a new thing, now it shall spring forth; shall you not know it? I will even make a road in the wilderness and rivers in the desert" (Isaiah 43:18–19).

"And they sang a new song, saying: 'You are worthy to take the scroll, And to open its seals; for You were slain, and have redeemed us to God by Your blood, out of every tribe and tongue and people and nation, and have made us kings and priests to our God; and we shall reign on the earth'" (Revelation 5:9–10).

PROPHETIC DECLARATION

I put on the whole armor of God. I am strong in the Lord and in the power of His might. I draw strength from the throne of grace to establish my dominion over every territorial power, in Jesus' name.

"For the kingdom is the LORD's, and He rules over the nations" (Psalm 22:28).

PRAYER POINTS

1. It is written: "For the kingdom is the Lord's; and He is the governor among the nations" (Psalm 22:28). My Lord Jesus Christ, rule in your power and might to scatter every strange kingdom attacking my life, in Jesus' name.

2. It is written: "And I will overthrow the throne of kingdoms, and I will destroy the strength of the kingdoms of the heathen; and I will overthrow the chariots, their riders shall come down" (Hag. 2:22, KJV). Therefore, every evil throne attacking my destiny, scatter asunder, in Jesus' name.

3. It is written: "The LORD has opened His armory, and has brought out the weapons of His indignation; for this is the work of the LORD God of hosts In the land" (Jeremiah 50:25). O Lord God of hosts, release your weapons of indignation to desolate the strongholds of the wicked attacking my life, in Jesus' name.

4. O east wind of God, scatter asunder every evil network set up against my life, in Jesus' name.

5. As the battle axe of God, I cut down every unprofitable tree in my life, in Jesus' name.

6. Every unprofitable tree in my life, be consumed by the Holy Spirit fire, in Jesus' name.

7. Every monitoring spirit assigned to cage my destiny, scatter asunder, in Jesus' name.

8. The vow of the wicked to frustrate my destiny, become an empty waste, in Jesus' name.

9. It is written: "He frustrates the devices of the crafty, So that their hands cannot carry out their plans" (Job 5:12). The craftiness of the wicked to keep me in bondage, let God arise and scatter them unto desolation, in Jesus' name.

10. Every evil mark and label in my life, be nullified and be destroyed by the blood of Jesus.

11. I decree the heavens and the gates of my environment open unto me now, in Jesus' name.

12. Give ear, O ye heavens, and heed unto my words O ye earth, henceforth, I possess the gates of my adversaries, in Jesus' name.

13. You, principalities and powers attached to my region, in the name of Jesus, I destroy your evil hold over my life.

14. You, the altar of darkness afflicting my region, be blasted asunder by the blood of Jesus.

15. It is written: "You will also declare a thing, and it will be established for you; so light will shine on your ways" (Job 22:28). Therefore, I decree the heavens of this nation to open unto me and great blessings to pour upon me now, in Jesus' name.

16. "The king's heart is in the hand of the LORD, like the rivers of water; He turns it wherever He wishes" (Proverbs 21:1). O Lord God, arise and touch the heart of the ruling class of this nation to my favor, in Jesus' name.

17. Every evil projection and manipulation against the leaders of this nation, be abolished by the blood of Jesus.

18. You, territorial powers and thrones attached to this nation in the name of Jesus you shall not waste my destiny.

19. My Lord Jesus Christ, you are my advocate and my mediator, plead favor and mercy on this nation in the heavenly courts, in Jesus' name.

20. In the name of Jesus, I receive the mantle of peace to possess the gates of this nation and to eat the good fruits thereof.

21. O voice of the blood of Jesus, speak restoration of peace unto this nation.

22. O breath of God, bring life unto this nation in Jesus name.

23. Blood of Jesus revisit the foundation of this nation and restore your glory, in Jesus' name.

24. Give thanks to God for answered prayers.

Day Eight

BREAKING FREE FROM EVIL SOUL TIES

"And the children of Israel said to them, 'Oh, that we had died by the hand of the LORD in the land of Egypt, when we sat by the pots of meat and when we ate bread to the full! For you have brought us out into this wilderness to kill this whole assembly with hunger.'"

(Exodus 16:3)

Many people find it difficult to experience freedom from relationships and associations of the past that hurt them. Something about their life is still strongly attached to the events of the past.

Life in Christ is refreshing and exciting. Enjoy it! It's time to break loose from evil ties that trouble and control your life.

Day Eight

BREAKING FREE FROM EVIL SOUL TIES

PRAISE AND WORSHIP
IT IS WRITTEN

I know that whatever God does, it shall be forever. Nothing can be added to it, and nothing taken from it. God does it, that men should fear before Him" (Ecclesiastes 3:14).

"Where the word of a king is, there is power; and who may say to him, 'What are you doing?'" (Ecclesiastes 8:4).

"Be shattered, O you peoples, and be broken in pieces! Give ear, all you from far countries. Gird yourselves, but be broken in pieces; Gird yourselves, but be broken in pieces. Take counsel together, but it will come to nothing; Speak the word, but it will not stand, for God is with us" (Isaiah 8:9–10).

"Woe to those who decree unrighteous decrees, who write misfortune, which they have prescribed" (Isaiah 10:1).

"Your covenant with death will be annulled, and your agreement with Sheol will not stand; when the overflowing scourge passes through, then you will be trampled down by it" (Isaiah 28:18).

"Come to Me, all you who labor and are heavy laden, and I will give you rest. Take My yoke upon you and learn from Me, for I am gentle and lowly in heart, and you will find rest for your souls. For My yoke is easy and My burden is light" (Matthew 11:28 30).

"Therefore, if anyone is in Christ, he is a new creation; old things have passed away; behold, all things have become new. Now all things are of God, who has reconciled us to Himself through Jesus Christ, and has given us the ministry of reconciliation, that is, that God was in Christ reconciling the world to Himself, not imputing their trespasses to them, and has committed to us the word of reconciliation. Now then, we are ambassadors for Christ, as though God were pleading through us: we implore you on Christ's behalf, be reconciled to God. For He made Him who knew no sin to be sin for us, that we might become the righteousness of God in Him" (2 Corinthians 5:17–21).

"If we say that we have no sin, we deceive ourselves, and the truth is not in us. If we confess our sins, He is faithful and just to forgive us our sins and to cleanse us from all unrighteousness. If we say that we have not sinned, we make Him a liar, and His word is not in us" (1 John 1:8–10).

"For whatever is born of God overcomes the world. And this is the victory that has overcome the world—our faith" (1 John 5:4).

PROPHETIC DECLARATION

It is written: "Can two walk together, except they be agreed?" (Amos 3:3). I repent of agreement or union that puts me in bondage and I plead the precious blood of Jesus to purge me. I renounce and denounce any relationship that brought evil upon me, in Jesus' name. I confess Jesus Christ as my Lord, Savior, Messiah and King. Jesus Christ my Redeemer is strong, the Lord of host is His name. He shall thoroughly plead my cause and set me free from all bondage.

PRAYER POINTS

1. Any conscious and unconscious evil agreement between me and anybody dead or alive be annulled by the blood of Jesus.

2. Witnesses to any evil covenant in my life, I proclaim your mandate terminated, in Jesus' name.

3. The summoning of my soul for evil be abolished by the blood of Jesus.

4. The captivity of darkness over my life due to my ignorance be terminated in the name of Jesus.

5. O arm of God, break asunder the strength of evil tie in my life, in Jesus' name.

6. Blood of Jesus, untie my destiny from bondage, in Jesus' name.

7. It is written: ". . . The right hand of the LORD does valiantly" (Psalm 118:16, NASB). Therefore, O Right Hand of God, desolate the stronghold of the wicked in my life, in Jesus' name.

8. I decree my destiny be withdrawn from the altars of the wicked, in Jesus' name.

9. By the blood of Jesus, I break free from inherited soul ties, in Jesus' name.

10. Anywhere my life has been fragmented for evil, O arm of God restore me to the fullness, in Jesus' name.

11. It is written: "It shall come to pass in that day that his burden will be taken away from your shoulder, and his yoke from your neck, and the yoke will be destroyed because of the anointing oil" (Isaiah 10:27). Therefore anointing of the Living God, destroy every evil yoke in my life, in Jesus' name.

12. Anointing of the Holy Spirit break me loose from all my captivities, in Jesus' name.

13. It is written: "Casting all your care upon Him, for He cares for you" (1 Peter 5:7). Therefore, any burden laid on my life to crush me, I cast you upon Jesus, in Jesus' name.

14. In the name of Jesus, I decree a fire of separation between me and an evil soul tie.

15. I decree to my soul, be set free from evil entanglement, in Jesus' name.

16. The curse of evil soul ties in my life break asunder, in Jesus' name.

17. Every imagination and thought, strengthening evil tie in my life, be consumed by the fire of the Holy Spirit, in Jesus' name.

18. In the name of Jesus, I bind my destiny to Jesus and the power of His blood.

19. Precious Holy Spirit, establish my relation in Jesus with wonderful testimonies, in Jesus' name.

20. O Lord God of Host, arise and rescue my soul from evil ties, in Jesus' name.

21. Evil consequences of soul tie covenants in my life be terminated by the blood of Jesus.

22. Every blessing that I have lost due to soul ties, blood of Jesus restore to me now, in Jesus' name.

23. It is written: "Therefore if the Son makes you free, you shall be free indeed" (John 8:36). Therefore, in the name of Jesus Christ, I am completely free from the captivities of evil soul tie.

24. Give thanks to God for answered prayers.

Day Nine
SOUND MIND AND SOUND VICTORY

"When Saul and all Israel heard these words of the Philistine, they were dismayed and greatly afraid."

(1 Samuel 17:11)

The race to greatness is not for the timid, neither is it for the cowards, nor for the fearful, but to those waxing strong in the midst of discouragement. Hindrances should not stop you; opposition should not weary you; they are all designed to promote and prosper you. A calm discipline and well-balanced mind is all you need for victory.

Day Nine
SOUND MIND AND SOUND VICTORY

PRAISE AND WORSHIP
IT IS WRITTEN

W hy are you cast down, O my soul? And why are you dis-
quieted within me? Hope in God, for I shall yet praise
Him for the help of His countenance" (Psalm 42:5).

"O God, my heart is steadfast; I will sing and give praise,
even with my glory" (Psalm 108:1).

"And He said to me, 'My grace is sufficient for you, for My
strength is made perfect in weakness.' Therefore most gladly
I will rather boast in my infirmities, that the power of Christ
may rest upon me" (2 Corinthians 12:9).

"And not in any way terrified by your adversaries, which is
to them a proof of perdition, but to you of salvation, and that
from God" (Philippians 1.28).

"For it is God who works in you both to will and to do for
His good pleasure" (Philippians 2:13).

"Brethren, I do not count myself to have apprehended; but
one thing I do, forgetting those things which are behind and
reaching forward to those things which are ahead, I press toward the goal for the prize of the upward call of God in Christ
Jesus" (Philippians 3:13–14).

"Rejoice in the Lord always. Again I will say, rejoice!" (Philippians 4:4).

"Now may the Lord of peace Himself give you peace always in every way. The Lord be with you all" (2 Thessalonians 3:16).

"For God has not given us a spirit of fear, but of power and of love and of a sound mind" (2 Timothy 1:7).

PROPHETIC DECLARATION

My knowing spirit and my feeling soul, be consecrated unto the Lord Most High for clarity of vision, in Jesus' name. I receive the grace to keep my heart with all diligence that pleasant and edifying things may spring forth, in Jesus' name.

A calm and well balanced mind to bring resounding victory is my portion, because I have the mind of Christ.

PRAYER POINTS

1. Blood of Jesus, flush bitterness and anguish out of my life, in Jesus' name.
2. Holy Spirit, saturate my thoughts and my intellect, in Jesus' name.
3. Blood of Jesus, heal me from emotional damage, in Jesus' name.
4. Fiery darts shot at my heart, lose hold, and vanish with your poisons, in Jesus' name.
5. Mind destructive demons, loosen me and flee, in Jesus' name.
6. The trading of my soul for evil be abolished by the blood of Jesus.
7. Evil stronghold in my mind, I cast you out, in Jesus' name.
8. By the quickening of the Holy Spirit, I overcome mind blankness, in Jesus' name.
9. In the name of Jesus, I overpower mind dullness.

10. Through the blood of Jesus, I subdue worries and anxieties, in Jesus' name.

11. Spirit of heaviness, flee from my life, in Jesus' name.

12. Guilt and condemnation flee from my life, in Jesus' name.

13. In the name of Jesus, I decree to my soul to escape the snare of oppression.

14. O Lord God, heal the blindness of my spirit man, in Jesus' name.

15. I bind the spirit of suicide and cast it out of my life, in Jesus' name.

16. In Jesus' name, my soul shall not suffer loss.

17. I enthrone Jesus as Lord over my body, soul and spirit, in Jesus' name.

18. Holy Spirit, strengthen my inner man with joy and peace, in Jesus' name.

19. Through the blood of Jesus, I consecrate my thoughts and imagination unto the Lord Most High, in Jesus' name.

20. I surrender my willpower to the lordship of Jesus Christ, in Jesus' name.

21. In the name of Jesus, I align my body, soul and spirit to God's purpose for my life.

22. Glory of the living God overwhelm my life, in Jesus' name.

23. O Lord God, assign your angels to guard my mind, in Jesus' name.

24. Give thanks to God for answered prayers.

Day Ten
FROM GENERATIONAL BONDAGES TO GENERATIONAL BLESSINGS

You've been held bound by evil effects of your family line, now is the time to reverse and correct it. Your family can have new and glorious beginning. You might have been noted for depression, affliction, and curses, but the good news is that with God at the center of your life; goodness, joy and the blessings shall yet abound. Therefore, arise and move from generational bondage to blessings.

"Now all these things happened to them as examples, and they were written for our admonition, upon whom the ends of the ages have come."

(1 Corinthians 10:11)

Day Ten

FROM GENERATIONAL BONDAGES TO GENERATIONAL BLESSINGS

PRAISE AND WORSHIP
IT IS WRITTEN

Happy are you, O Israel! Who is like you, a people saved by the LORD, the shield of your help and the sword of your majesty! Your enemies shall submit to you, and you shall tread down their high places" (Deuteronomy 33:29).

"This is Jacob, the generation of those who seek Him, who seek Your face" (Psalm 24:6).

"Here am I and the children whom the LORD has given me! We are for signs and wonders in Israel from the LORD of hosts, Who dwells in Mount Zion" (Isaiah 8:18).

"Your covenant with death will be annulled, and your agreement with Sheol will not stand; When the overflowing scourge passes through, then you will be trampled down by it" (Isaiah 28:18).

"For your Maker is your husband, The LORD of hosts is His name; and your Redeemer is the Holy One of Israel; He is called the God of the whole earth" (Isaiah 54:5).

"'Your fierceness has deceived you, the pride of your heart, O you who dwell in the clefts of the rock, who hold the height of the hill! Though you make your nest as high as the eagle, I will bring you down from there,' says the LORD" (Jeremiah 49:16).

"Their Redeemer is strong; The LORD of hosts is His name. He will thoroughly plead their case, that He may give rest to the land, and disquiet the inhabitants of Babylon" (Jeremiah 50:34).

"Do you not know that you are the temple of God and that the Spirit of God dwells in you? If anyone defiles the temple of God, God will destroy him. For the temple of God is holy, which temple you are" (1 Corinthians 3:16–17).

"For we do not have a High Priest who cannot sympathize with our weaknesses, but was in all points tempted as we are, yet without sin. Let us therefore come boldly to the throne of grace, that we may obtain mercy and find grace to help in time of need" (Hebrews 4:15–16).

PROPHETIC DECLARATION

I come boldly before the Shekinah presence of the living God to stand in the gap for my family line to receive appropriate and well-timed help. My generation stands in awe of Your work and declares Your mighty acts, even Your wonderful works. Therefore, let there be revelation of Your majestic, glorious splendor and wonderful miracles on my family line, in Jesus' name.

PRAYER POINTS

1. Blood of Jesus, redeem my birthright, in Jesus' name.
2. Afflictions and sorrows are not my lot, so I reject them, in Jesus' name.
3. I bind with fetters of fire, the strongman attached to my heritage, in Jesus' name.
4. O Lord God, order my steps out of every captivity, in Jesus' name.
5. Forces of affliction and oppression on my divine heritage wither now, in Jesus' name.

6. Every evil guard attached to my family lineage, be dispossessed and scattered, in the name of Jesus.

7. Blood of Jesus, detach me from the bondage of my hometown, in Jesus' name.

8. Every satanic strongman attached to my family line, be subdued by the blood of Jesus.

9. Blood of Jesus, destroy every evil family pattern operating in my life, in Jesus' name.

10. O right hand of God, pull me out of every evil family coverage, in Jesus' name.

11. I break covenant with any family idol and shrine, in Jesus' name.

12. I recall my conception and I challenge it with the Holy Spirit fire, in Jesus' name.

13. I recall the time I spent in the womb, and I challenge it with the Holy Spirit fire, in Jesus' name.

14. Holy Spirit fire, deliver me from every placenta bondage, in Jesus' name.

15. By the blood of Jesus, I destroy every evil blood covenant affecting my life, in Jesus' name.

16. I recall all my developmental stages [time of learning to sit, crawl, stand, walk, run, talk, cry, and eat] and I challenge them by the Holy Spirit fire, in Jesus' name.

17. Every evil flow of breast milk from a polluted breast into my life, be flushed out by the blood of Jesus.

18. I decree fire of separation between me and my generational bondage, in Jesus' name.

19. Blood of Jesus, destroy every evil generational mark in my life, in Jesus' name.

20. Any affliction in my life as a result of evil generational networks, be terminated by the Holy Spirit fire, in Jesus' name.

21. Blessings due to my family line manifest now in me, in Jesus' name.

22. Holy Spirit, redefine my life to suit my divine destiny, in Jesus' name.
23. I covenant my family line in the blood of Jesus for peace, joy and blessings, in Jesus' name.
24. Give thanks to God for answered prayers.

BREAKING LOOSE AND BREAKING FREE

Freedom is not free until you are totally liberated out of the control of opposing forces. You have for a long time been restrained, held back and deprived of joyful and peaceful living. Step out of your confinement and enjoy the freedom in Christ Jesus. Be determined as you pray this prayer that true freedom shall be your portion, in Jesus' name.

"So the LORD saved Israel that day out of the hand of the Egyptians, and Israel saw the Egyptians dead on the seashore."

(Exodus 14:30)

Day Eleven

BREAKING LOOSE AND BREAKING FREE

PRAISE AND WORSHIP
IT IS WRITTEN

And Miriam answered them: 'Sing to the LORD, for He has triumphed gloriously! The horse and its rider He has thrown into the sea!'" (Exodus 15:21).

"Surely He shall deliver you from the snare of the fowler and from the perilous pestilence" (Psalm 91:3).

"Our soul has escaped as a bird from the snare of the fowlers; The snare is broken, and we have escaped" (Psalm 124:7).

"Bring my soul out of prison, that I may praise Your name; The righteous shall surround me, for You shall deal bountifully with me" (Psalm 142:7).

"Therefore if the Son makes you free, you shall be free indeed" (John 8:36).

"And they glorified God in me" (Galatians 1:24).

"But when the fullness of the time had come, God sent forth His Son, born of a woman, born under the law, to redeem those who were under the law, that we might receive the adoption as sons. And because you are sons, God has sent forth the Spirit of His Son into your hearts, crying out, 'Abba, Father!'

Therefore you are no longer a slave but a son, and if a son, then an heir of God through Christ" (Galatians 4:4 7).

"Stand fast therefore in the liberty by which Christ has made us free, and do not be entangled again with a yoke of bondage" (Galatians 5:1).

"From now on let no one trouble me, for I bear in my body the marks of the Lord Jesus. Brethren, the grace of our Lord Jesus Christ be with your spirit. Amen" (Galatians 6:17–18).

PROPHETIC DECLARATION

Christ Jesus has completely liberated me from sin and from the world of darkness. I therefore, withdraw my submission to oppression, hardship and affliction, in Jesus' name.

Evil shall no longer exert dominion over me, because I am subject to God's favor and mercy.

PRAYER POINTS

1. O blood of Jesus, cleanse me, purge me and make me whole, in Jesus' name.
2. Blood of Jesus that knows no impossibility, blast asunder every yoke of affliction in my life, in Jesus' name.
3. Every internal altar programmed in my life to afflict me, in the name of Jesus, loosen your hold and vanish.
4. Every verdict of darkness on my life, Almighty God, the Judge of heaven and earth, desolate it now, in Jesus' name.
5. The scepter of the wicked pointed at me in judgment, be withdrawn and perish, in Jesus' name.
6. The seat of the wicked watching over my destiny, scatter, in Jesus' name.
7. The claims of the wicked over my life be abolished by the blood of Jesus, in Jesus' name.
8. Any area of my life that I have lost control unto the enemies, by the blood of Jesus, I dispossess the enemies and I gain back the control, in Jesus' name.

9. Wherever I have been sold out unto captivity, O redemptive blood of Jesus, buy me back, in Jesus' name.

10. Afflictions passed down to me by my parents, precious blood of Jesus, annul, abolish and desolate them, in Jesus' name.

11. You, mind-controlling demons, loosen your hold over my life, flee and never return, in Jesus' name.

12. O thunder tempest of God, strike down the high places of my oppressors, in Jesus' name.

13. Anything that has been taken from my life to attack me, blood of Jesus, withdraw it and set me free, in Jesus' name.

14. It is written: ". . . the desire of the wicked shall perish" (Psalm 112:10). Therefore, the desires of the wicked for my life perish, in the name of Jesus.

15. In the name of Jesus, I proclaim the dominion of the wicked over my life to become an empty waste.

16. In the name of Jesus, I command the fury of the mighty targeted at me to turn back upon their own heads.

17. It is written: "As for the head of those who surround me, Let the evil of their lips cover them" (Psalm 140:9). Therefore, every mischief targeted at me, turn back and be fulfilled upon my adversaries, in Jesus' name.

18. Holy Spirit, guide the affairs of my life and lead me to greatness, in Jesus' name.

19. Anointing to break loose and break free from bondages, manifest in my now, in Jesus' name.

20. My Lord Jesus Christ, you're the light of the world, therefore, let Your light arise and shine in my darkness, in Jesus' name.

21. By the blood of Jesus Christ, I entrench my dominion and supremacy over all wicked works, in Jesus' name.

22. By the blood of Jesus, I break loose and break free from generational limitations, in Jesus' name.

23. I break loose and break free from problems unto divine solutions, in Jesus' name.
24. Give thanks to God for answered prayers.

Day Twelve
DELIVER US FROM EVIL

"Each day has enough trouble of its own."
(Matthew 6:34, NIV)

We are in an age when people are addicted to evil, but allergic to good. God will surely deliver you from the angry turmoil and keep you secure in Him. Never yield to evil. This prayer section is a protective shield over your life.

Day Twelve

DELIVER US FROM EVIL

PRAISE AND WORSHIP
IT IS WRITTEN

Oh, let the wickedness of the wicked come to an end, but establish the just; For the righteous God tests the hearts and minds" (Psalm 7:9).

"God is a just judge, and God is angry with the wicked every day" (Psalm 7:11).

"The righteous is delivered from trouble, and it comes to the wicked instead" (Proverbs 11:8).

"The evil will bow before the good, and the wicked at the gates of the righteous" (Proverbs 14:19).

"And do not lead us into temptation, but deliver us from the evil one. For Yours is the kingdom and the power and the glory forever. Amen" (Matthew 6:13).

"I do not pray that You should take them out of the world, but that You should keep them from the evil one" (John 17:15).

"From now on let no one trouble me, for I bear in my body the marks of the Lord Jesus" (Galatians 6:17).

"And the Lord will deliver me from every evil work and preserve me for His heavenly kingdom. To Him be glory forever and ever. Amen!" (2 Timothy 4:18).

"Then the Lord knows how to deliver the godly out of temptations and to reserve the unjust under punishment for the day of judgment" (2 Peter 2:9).

PROPHETIC DECLARATION

Thus says the Lord God of Host unto me, "The LORD has taken away your judgments, He has cast out your enemy. The King of Israel, the LORD, is in your midst; you shall see disaster no more" (Zephaniah 3:15), in Jesus' name. Through the triumphant death and resurrection of my Lord Jesus Christ, the power of evil has lost its grip over my life. Therefore, there's nothing to fear from evil again, in Jesus' name.

PRAYER POINTS

1. In the name of Jesus, the power of evil shall not corrupt my destiny.
2. As it is written: "Be pleased, O LORD, to deliver me; O LORD, make haste to help me!" (Psalm 40:13).
3. It is written: "But Jesus, knowing their thoughts, said, "Why do you think evil in your hearts?" (Matthew 9:4). Therefore, any power, spirit or personality thinking evil against me, become an empty waste, in Jesus' name.
4. Blood of Jesus, uproot and desolate the evil planted in my foundation.
5. As the Lord God of Host lives and as His Spirit lives, evil shall no longer invade my life, in Jesus' name.
6. Blood of Jesus, disconnect me from inherited evil, in Jesus' name.
7. Through the blood of Jesus, I overcome the fear of evil, in Jesus' name.
8. Evil sown into my family line, dry up now, in Jesus' name.

9. Evil agents, be subdued before me and flee, in Jesus' name.

10. Any power, spirit or personality covenanted and empowered by evil, shall not prevail against me, in Jesus' name.

11. Holy Spirit, lift up a standard of desolation against the pursuit of evil in my life, in Jesus' name.

12. Evil projected into the work of creation against my life, shall not prosper, in Jesus' name.

13. Anointing of the Holy Spirit, destroy the yoke of evil in my life, in Jesus' name.

14. I reject and eject any and every evil planting in my life, by the blood of Jesus, in Jesus' name.

15. My senses and organs, be purged from evil, in Jesus' name.

16. In the name of Jesus, henceforth, no evil thought shall prevail in my life.

17. Any evil ever done to me, be converted to good by the blood of Jesus.

18. Every evil authority over my life, come to naught, in Jesus' name.

19. In the name of Jesus, I break free from evil associations and agreements.

20. In the name of Jesus, my blessings shall not be corrupted by evil.

21. Blood of Jesus, sanctify the days of my life that no evil will manifest, in Jesus' name.

22. In the name of Jesus, I decree fire of separation between me and evil.

23. Thanks be to God for giving me victory over evil, in Jesus' name.

24. Give thanks to God for answered prayer.

Day Thirteen
OVERCOMING
DREAM ATTACKS

"But while men slept, his enemy came and sowed tares among the wheat and went his way . . . He said to them, 'An enemy has done this.' The servants said to him, 'Do you want us then to go and gather them up?'"

(Matthew 13:25, 28)

Your dream life should be a stream of divine visions and revelations, but this is not the case with many people.

Think of those times when you had a sound sleep without nightmares. Nightmares are a horrible experience for many because of evil visitations, evil plantings and soul trafficking. Attacks in dreams have resulted in unexplainable sicknesses and diseases in many lives. Through the blood of Jesus, you can reverse and annul them. Enough of evil manipulation in your dream life! Claim your victory and your sleep shall be sweet.

(Proverbs 3:24)

Day Thirteen
OVERCOMING
DREAM ATTACKS

PRAISE AND WORSHIP
IT IS WRITTEN

Why do the nations rage, and the people plot a vain thing? The kings of the earth set themselves, and the rulers take counsel together against the LORD and against His Anointed, saying, 'Let us break their bonds in pieces and cast away their cords from us.' He who sits in the heavens shall laugh; The Lord shall hold them in derision. Then He shall speak to them in His wrath, and distress them in His deep displeasure" (Psalm 2:1–5).

"Let God arise, let His enemies be scattered; Let those also who hate Him flee before Him. As smoke is driven away, so drive them away; As wax melts before the fire, So let the wicked perish at the presence of God. But let the righteous be glad; Let them rejoice before God; Yes, let them rejoice exceedingly" (Psalm 68:1–3).

"Thus says the Lord GOD: 'It shall not stand, nor shall it come to pass'" (Isaiah 7:7).

"Scarcely shall they be planted, scarcely shall they be sown, scarcely shall their stock take root in the earth, when He will also blow on them, and they will wither, and the whirlwind will take them away like stubble" (Isaiah 40:2).

"Who is he who speaks and it comes to pass, when the Lord has not commanded it?" (Lamentations 3:37).

"He reveals deep and secret things; He knows what is in the darkness, and light dwells with Him" (Daniel 2:22).

"The king answered Daniel, and said, 'Truly your God is the God of gods, the Lord of kings, and a revealer of secrets, since you could reveal this secret'" (Daniel 2:47).

"If that is the case, our God whom we serve is able to deliver us from the burning fiery furnace, and He will deliver us from your hand, O king" (Daniel 3:17).

"And even now the ax is laid to the root of the trees. Therefore every tree which does not bear good fruit is cut down and thrown into the fire" (Matthew 3:10).

PROPHETIC DECLARATION

Thank you my Lord Jesus Christ because you're not the author of confusion, but the author and finisher of my faith (Hebrews 12:2). I boldly declare that in the name of Jesus Christ, I shall not sleep the sleep of death, but my sleep shall be sweet and refreshing. It shall be a divine revelation and not an evil visitation. Thank you my Lord Jesus Christ, for revealing Yourself unto me.

PRAYER POINTS

1. By the blood of Jesus, I break asunder every evil dream covenant in my life, in Jesus' name.
2. In the name of Jesus, I come against the spirit of heaviness and I cast it out of my life.
3. I declare that the slumber spirit shall not overwhelm my soul, in Jesus' name.
4. Evil summoning power over my soul, be bound and be of non-effect, in Jesus' name.

5. You, army of darkness, assigned against my life, be swallowed up by the Lord God of Host, in Jesus' name.

6. Every gathering of the oppressors against my soul, be overwhelmed with confusion and desolation, in Jesus' name.

7. The tormentors of my good sleep be bound and be slain by your torments, in Jesus' name.

8. Every weapon fired at me in my sleep, come out now, with all your poisons, in Jesus' name.

9. The cycle of evil dream(s) in my life, be broken asunder, in Jesus' name.

10. The vehicle of captivity in my life, be burnt to ashes, in Jesus' name.

11. Dream manipulation of my destiny, be annulled by the blood of Jesus.

12. Attack by the spirit of death and hell in my dream(s), be abolished by the blood of Jesus.

13. Angels of the living God, break me loose from every dream imprisonment, in Jesus' name.

14. The throne and palaces of darkness ruling over my life, O heavens, smite them to desolation, in Jesus' name.

15. My glory and blessings tied down in the dream world be reconciled unto me by the blood of Jesus.

16. Through the blood of Jesus, I overcome dream pollution, in Jesus' name.

17. I decree my bed to be an altar unto the Most High God, the Holy One of Israel, for divine visitations, in Jesus' name.

18. Sickness and diseases in my life, through dreams, be healed by the blood of Jesus, in Jesus' name.

19. I covenant my dream life to the precious blood of Jesus and the power of the Holy Spirit, in Jesus' name.

20. O Lord God Almighty, assign your holy angels to guide my dream life, in Jesus' name.

21. Every good dream that I have ever had, I decree you to come to manifestation now, in Jesus' name.
22. Henceforth, I prophesy to my dream life to be full of divine information to profit my life, in Jesus' name.
23. The awakening out of my sleep, be quickened by the power of the Holy Spirit unto abundant life, in Jesus' name.
24. Give thanks to God for answered prayers.

Day Fourteen

DISMANTLING THE HOLD OF FAMILIAR SPIRIT

The familiar spirit is a spirit that is well acquainted and intimate with an environment, a family line or association. The spirit is well-informed even unto the deepest secret. It holds record of events and occurrences in a family line or in an environment. It is a demon spirit possessing mediums, making predictions. It promotes enchantments, witchcraft, sorcery, sooth-saying and necromancy

"And the person who turns to mediums and familiar spirits, to prostitute himself with them, I will set My face against that person and cut him off from his people."

(Lev. 20:6)

Day Fourteen

DISMANTLING THE HOLD OF FAMILIAR SPIRIT

PRAISE AND WORSHIP
IT IS WRITTEN

"Give no regard to mediums and familiar spirits; do not seek after them, to be defiled by them: I am the LORD your God" (Lev. 19:31).

"'A man or a woman who is a medium, or who has familiar spirits, shall surely be put to death; they shall stone them with stones. Their blood shall be upon them'" (Lev. 20:27).

"Shall the prey be taken from the mighty, or the captives of the righteous be delivered? But thus says the LORD: 'Even the captives of the mighty shall be taken away, and the prey of the terrible be delivered; For I will contend with him who contends with you, and I will save your children. I will feed those who oppress you with their own flesh, and they shall be drunk with their own blood as with sweet wine. All flesh shall know that I, the LORD, am your Savior, and your Redeemer, the Mighty One of Jacob'" (Isaiah 49:24–26).

"See, I have this day set you over the nations and over the kingdoms, to root out and to pull down, to destroy and to throw down, to build and to plant" (Jeremiah 1:10).

"But if I cast out demons with the finger of God, surely the kingdom of God has come upon you. When a strong man, fully armed, guards his own palace, his goods are in peace. But when a stronger than he comes upon him and overcomes him, he takes from him all his armor in which he trusted, and divides his spoils" (Luke 11:20–22).

"In the beginning was the Word, and the Word was with God, and the Word was God. He was in the beginning with God. All things were made through Him, and without Him nothing was made that was made. In Him was life, and the life was the light of men. And the light shines in the darkness, and the darkness did not comprehend it" (John 1:1–5).

"Therefore God also has highly exalted Him and given Him the name which is above every name, that at the name of Jesus every knee should bow, of those in heaven, and of those on earth, and of those under the earth, and that every tongue should confess that Jesus Christ is Lord, to the glory of God the Father" (Philippians 2:9–11).

"He has delivered us from the power of darkness and conveyed us into the kingdom of the Son of His love, in whom we have redemption through His blood, the forgiveness of sins. He is the image of the invisible God, the firstborn over all creation. For by Him all things were created that are in heaven and that are on earth, visible and invisible, whether thrones or dominions or principalities or powers. All things were created through Him and for Him. And He is before all things, and in Him all things consist" (Colossians 1:13–17).

"He who leads into captivity shall go into captivity; he who kills with the sword must be killed with the sword. Here is the patience and the faith of the saints" (Revelation 13:10).

PROPHETIC DECLARATION

"You will show me the path of life; In Your presence is fullness of joy; At Your right hand are pleasures forevermore"

(Psalm 16:11). Therefore, O Lord my God, let the joy and the pleasure of Your presence overwhelm me.

By the ordinances that made the heavens and the earth, I entrench my dominion and my superiority in the realm of the spirit, by the blood of Jesus.

Therefore, I call for re-enforcement of Holy Angels to execute and bring to pass the pronouncement of my mouth, in Jesus' name.

You, Angels of the Living God, that excel in strength, minister strength and fulfillment to me now, in Jesus' name.

PRAYER POINTS

1. Every family idol pulling me back to captivity, it is written: "They are vanity, and the work of errors; In the time of their visitation they shall perish" (Jeremiah 10:15). Therefore, I command you to perish, in Jesus' name.

2. You, the gods and the goddesses demanding worship and set to put me in captivity, thus saith the LORD God of Host unto you: "But the LORD is the true God, he is the living God, and an everlasting King: at his wrath the earth shall tremble, and the nations shall not be able to abide his indignation. Thus shall ye say unto them, the gods that have not made the heavens and the earth, even they shall perish from the earth, and from under these heavens" (Jeremiah 10:10–11, KJV). Therefore, I command you to perish, in Jesus' name.

3. You, foundational wicked elders, come under the arrest of the Holy Spirit, in Jesus' name.

4. You, diviners set up against me, hear your eternal judgment, it is written: "Who frustrates the signs of the babblers, and drives diviners mad; Who turns wise men backward, and makes their knowledge foolishness"

(Isaiah 44:25). Therefore, be smitten by the LORD God of Host, in Jesus' name.

5. Every network of witchcraft and familiar spirits afflicting my life, shatter, in Jesus' name.

6. Any evil visitation that has led me into bondage, be abolished, in Jesus' name.

7. You, cycle of failure, defeat and shame in my life, be desolated now, in Jesus' name.

8. You, yoke of confusion in my life, perish now, in Jesus' name.

9. Every omen, evil marks and labels in my life, be blotted out now, by the blood of Jesus Christ, in Jesus' name.

10. Whatever may be magnetizing evil into my life, melt out now, in Jesus' name.

11. Every conspiracy and mischief targeted at me, become an empty waste now, in Jesus' name.

12. Environmental familiar spirit, I subdue you by the blood of Jesus, in Jesus' name.

13. The evil spirits assigned to my paternal and maternal lines, your assignments are terminated, in Jesus' name.

14. Every evil monitoring spirit, evil eyes and evil networking against my life, perish now, in Jesus' name.

15. My blessings tied down by familiar spirits, be set free, in Jesus' name.

16. Anyone under any demonic influence that has vowed to make me a prey be arrested and become your own prey, in Jesus' name.

17. The gate keepers permitting evil trafficking into my life, give up and be made desolate, in Jesus' name.

18. No evil dedications and rituals in my environment shall prosper, in Jesus' name.

19. I enthrone Jesus Christ as Lord and King over my family line, in Jesus' name.

20. Every battle of familiar spirits raging at me, O Lord God of Host, quench it, in Jesus' name.

21. My divinely ordained destiny, be restored unto me now, in Jesus' name.

22. Lord God, ordain Your mighty angels, to violently withdraw all my blessings tied down to the altars of familiar spirits, in the name of Jesus.

23. Every re-enforcement of familiar spirits against my life, be blasted asunder by the blood of Jesus.

24. Give thanks to God for answered prayers.

Day Fifteen
VICTORY OVER DEPRESSION

The cares and burdens of this world are enough to crush your spirit and push you to a state of despondency. Depression is increasing. Sad to say, it will become worse toward the end of the age, but you can surely overcome it as you cast all your care upon Jesus.

"Casting all your care upon Him, for He cares for you."

(1 Peter 5:7)

Day Fifteen
VICTORY OVER DEPRESSION

PRAISE AND WORSHIP
IT IS WRITTEN

In the beginning God created the heavens and the earth. The earth was without form, and void; and darkness was on the face of the deep. And the Spirit of God was hovering over the face of the waters. Then God said, 'Let there be light'; and there was light" (Genesis 1:1–3).

"And the light shines in the darkness, and the darkness did not comprehend it" (John 1:5).

"There is therefore now no condemnation to those who are in Christ Jesus, who do not walk according to the flesh, but according to the Spirit" (Romans 8:1).

"Casting down arguments and every high thing that exalts itself against the knowledge of God, bringing every thought into captivity to the obedience of Christ" (2 Corinthians 10:5).

"Be anxious for nothing, but in everything by prayer and supplication, with thanksgiving, let your requests be made known to God; and the peace of God, which surpasses all understanding, will guard your hearts and minds through Christ Jesus" (Philippians 4:6–7).

"For the word of God is living and powerful, and sharper than any two-edged sword, piercing even to the division of soul and spirit, and of joints and marrow, and is a discerner of the thoughts and intents of the heart" (Hebrews 4:12).

"Therefore submit to God. Resist the devil and he will flee from you" (James 4:7).

"Casting all your care upon Him, for He cares for you" (1 Peter 5:7).

PROPHETIC DECLARATION

My Lord Jesus Christ, I enthrone your majesty in my life. I boldly declare that Jesus Christ rules in me and His reign is eternal. By the blood of Jesus, I stand against the robbers of my faith, peace, and trust. In the name of Jesus, I renounce and reject any weight tormenting my soul. Hear, O heaven and earth, nothing shall depress me any longer, but I shall ever live in dominion and in the joy of the Holy Spirit.

PRAYER POINTS

1. Blood of Jesus, heal my wounded spirit, in the name of Jesus.
2. Any poison projected into my soul, be flushed out by the blood of Jesus.
3. In the name of Jesus, I subdue my emotions.
4. Precious Holy Spirit, rule over my emotions, in Jesus' name.
5. You mind controlling demons, loose your hold over my life and flee, in Jesus' name.
6. Every suicidal manipulation of my thought, I bind you and cast you out, in Jesus' name.
7. Blood of Jesus, deliver me from mood disorder.
8. Every cycle of rejection, abandonment and hopelessness in my life, I command you to break asunder, in Jesus' name.

9. Every cycle of worthlessness, anxiety and worries in my life, I command you to break asunder, in Jesus' name.

10. Blood of Jesus, deliver me from mental torture, in Jesus' name.

11. Every sense of inadequacy, be flushed out of my life, in Jesus' name.

12 You, strongman of depression, I bind and cast you out of my life with your strongholds, in Jesus' name.

13. The torments of my past failures and defeats, be converted to victories and praises, in Jesus' name.

14. Every environmental threat over my soul, in the name of Jesus, be blasted asunder.

15. Every summoning of my soul to evil, be annulled by the blood of Jesus.

16. In the name of Jesus, I cast my burdens on my Lord and Savior, Jesus Christ.

17. Every cloud of confusion on my soul, I cast you unto desolation, in Jesus' name.

18. Precious Holy Spirit, minister life unto every area of my life, in Jesus' name.

19. Angels of the living God, cast down every stumbling block to my progress in life, in Jesus' name.

20. Precious Holy Spirit, transform my thoughts and my imaginations, in Jesus' name.

21. Henceforth no flood of the enemy shall break down my defenses, in Jesus' name.

22. Blood of Jesus, heal the root of depression in my life, in Jesus' name.

23. By the blood of Jesus, I break free from inherited depression, in Jesus' name.

24. Give thanks to God, in Jesus' name.

Day Sixteen

TURNING CURSES TO BLESSINGS

Blessings are stronger and more powerful than curses. A curse might have been invoked to afflict you, but it can be broken. Christ Jesus has purchased your freedom from doom, becoming cursed to annul your curse.

"Christ has redeemed us from the curse of the law, having become a curse for us (for it is written: 'Cursed is everyone who hangs on a tree'), that the blessing of Abraham might come upon the Gentiles in Christ Jesus, that we might receive the promise of the Spirit through faith."

(Galatians 3:13–14)

Day Sixteen
TURNING CURSES TO BLESSINGS

PRAISE AND WORSHIP
IT IS WRITTEN

B ut as for you, you meant evil against me; but God meant it for good, in order to bring it about as it is this day, to save many people alive" (Genesis 50:20).

"But the children of Israel were fruitful and increased abundantly, multiplied and grew exceedingly mighty; and the land was filled with them" (Exodus 1:7).

"How shall I curse whom God has not cursed? And how shall I denounce whom the LORD has not denounced? . . . For there is no sorcery against Jacob, nor any divination against Israel. It now must be said of Jacob and of Israel, 'Oh, what God has done!' Look, a people rises like a lioness, and lifts itself up like a lion; It shall not lie down until it devours the prey, and drinks the blood of the slain" (Numbers 23:8, 23–24).

"Nevertheless the LORD your God would not listen to Balaam, but the LORD your God turned the curse into a blessing for you, because the LORD your God loves you" (Deuteronomy 23:5).

"There is no one like the God of Jeshurun, Who rides the heavens to help you, And in His excellency on the clouds. The eternal God is your refuge, and underneath are the everlasting arms; He will thrust out the enemy from before you, And will say, 'Destroy!'" (Deuteronomy 33:26–27).

"Because they had not met the children of Israel with bread and water, but hired Balaam against them to curse them. However, our God turned the curse into a blessing" (Nehemiah 13:2).

"For the Lord GOD will help Me; Therefore I will not be disgraced; Therefore I have set My face like a flint, And I know that I will not be ashamed. He is near who justifies Me; Who will contend with Me? Let us stand together. Who is My adversary? Let him come near Me. Surely the Lord GOD will help Me; Who is he who will condemn Me? Indeed they will all grow old like a garment; The moth will eat them up" (Isaiah 50:7–9).

"'Indeed they shall surely assemble, but not because of Me. Whoever assembles against you shall fall for your sake. Behold, I have created the blacksmith who blows the coals in the fire, who brings forth an instrument for his work; And I have created the spoiler to destroy. No weapon formed against you shall prosper, and every tongue which rises against you in judgment you shall condemn. This is the heritage of the servants of the LORD, and their righteousness is from Me,' says the LORD" (Isaiah 54:15–17).

"Behold, I give you the authority to trample on serpents and scorpions, and over all the power of the enemy, and nothing shall by any means hurt you" (Luke 10:19).

"Christ has redeemed us from the curse of the law, having become a curse for us (for it is written: 'Cursed is everyone who hangs on a tree'), that the blessing of Abraham might come upon the Gentiles in Christ Jesus, that we might receive the promise of the Spirit through faith" (Galatians 3:13–14).

PROPHETIC DECLARATION

Thanks be to God who has delivered me from all bondage and afflictions through Christ Jesus my Lord. Through the death and resurrection of Jesus, I triumph over curses. I boldly declare that henceforth, curses shall no longer reign in my life, in Jesus' name. I have passed from curses to blessings and from troubles into peace and joy in the Holy Spirit. God, who commanded the light to shine out of darkness, has called me out of curses into blessings, in Jesus' name.

PRAYER POINTS

1. It is written: "And no marvel; for Satan himself is transformed into an angel of light" (2 Corinthians 11:14, KJV). Therefore, any power, spirit or personality under Satanic transformation to curse me, be bound and be silenced, in Jesus' name.
2. Every fiery dart of curses against me, be quenched, in Jesus' name.
3. Every flaming missile targeted at me, be extinguished by the blood of Jesus.
4. Every attack of the devourer and destroyer on my life shall not prosper, in Jesus' name.
5. It is written: "For if God spared not the angels that sinned, but cast them down to hell, and delivered them into chains of darkness, to be reserved unto judgment;" (2 Peter 2:4, KJV). Therefore, my Almighty Father, spare not the destruction of hired cursers mandated against me, in Jesus' name.
6. The spirits and powers energizing curses in my life, be subdued by the terror of God, in Jesus' name.
7. The oracle behind curses in my life, perish, in Jesus' name.
8. It is written: "And out of his mouth went a sharp two-edged sword . . ." (Revelation 1:16, KJV). It is also

written, "And will fight against them with the sword of my mouth" (Revelation 2:16, KJV). Therefore, my Lord Jesus Christ, let the sword of Thy mouth slay the hired cursers set at me, in Jesus' name.

9. Blood of Jesus, abolish generational curses operating in my life, in Jesus' name.

10. Every evil record keeper of my life, be subdued by the terror of God, in Jesus' name.

11. Thus says the Lord God of Host to all curses manifesting in my life, "The Lord will be terrible unto them; for He will famish all the gods" (Zephaniah 2:11, KJV) in Jesus' name.

12. Let the Angel of the Lord stand in the way as an adversary against hired curses set at me, in Jesus' name.

13. Anything within and around me operating under curses, be set free now, in the name of Jesus.

14. My Lord Jesus Christ, my merciful and faithful high priest, turn every curse in my life to blessing, in Jesus' name.

15. My Lord Jesus Christ, who ever lives to make intercession for me, arise now and turn every curse on my life into blessings, in Jesus' name.

16. And I called on the God of Israel saying, "Oh, that You would bless me indeed, and enlarge my territory, that Your hand would be with me, and that You would keep *me* from evil, that I may not cause pain! So God granted me what I requested, in Jesus' name" (1 Chronicles 4:10).

17. O Lord Most High God, let Your eternal weight of glory overwhelm my life now, in Jesus' name.

18. I proclaim, before the God of heaven and earth, that henceforth, no curse, no spell, nor enchantment would ever manifest in my life, in Jesus' name.

19. It is written: "And it shall come to pass in that day, that his burden shall be taken away from off thy neck, and the yoke shall be destroyed because of the anointing" (Isaiah 10:27, KJV). Therefore, I decree the anointing of the Holy Spirit to destroy every curse in my life, in Jesus' name.
20. Precious blood of Jesus, repel curses from my life, in Jesus' name.
21. Any curse covering my glory, be removed and be set ablaze, in Jesus' name.
22. O Lord God of Abraham, Isaac and Jacob, arise and exalt my head with honor in Jesus' name.
23. My scattered and transferred blessings, come forth unto me now, in Jesus' name.
24. Give thanks to God for answered prayers.

Day Seventeen
Un-caging My Glory

"There is one glory of the sun, another glory of the moon, and another glory of the stars; for one star differs from another star in glory."

(1 Corinthians 15:41)

You are a treasured possession, ordained by God to prosper. There is a glory in you that the whole world is waiting to see. This prayer session will surely cause the glory to emerge suddenly.

Day Seventeen

UN-CAGING MY GLORY

PRAISE AND WORSHIP
IT IS WRITTEN

He frustrates the devices of the crafty, so that their hands cannot carry out their plans" (Job 5:12).

"For You, O LORD, will bless the righteous; with favor You will surround him as with a shield" (Psalm 5:12).

"For He spoke, and it was done; He commanded, and it stood fast. The LORD brings the counsel of the nations to nothing; He makes the plans of the peoples of no effect. The counsel of the LORD stands forever, the plans of His heart to all generations" (Psalm 33:9–11).

"Evil shall slay the wicked, and those who hate the righteous shall be condemned" (Psalm 34:21).

"When I cry out to You, then my enemies will turn back; This I know, because God is for me" (Psalm 56:9).

"Blessed be the LORD, Who has not given us as prey to their teeth. Our soul has escaped as a bird from the snare of the fowlers; The snare is broken, and we have escaped. Our help is in the name of the LORD, Who made heaven and earth" (Psalm 124:6–8).

"'The pride of your heart has deceived you, you who dwell in the clefts of the rock, whose habitation is high; You who say in your heart, "Who will bring me down to the ground?" Though you ascend as high as the eagle, and though you set your nest among the stars, from there I will bring you down,' says the LORD" (Obadiah 3–4).

"The LORD will be awesome to them, for He will reduce to nothing all the gods of the earth; People shall worship Him, each one from his place, indeed all the shores of the nations" (Zephaniah 2:11).

PROPHETIC DECLARATION

I am a chaste bride of Christ, purchased and redeemed by the precious blood of Jesus. I have been rescued from the dominion of darkness and translated to the Kingdom of Light in Christ Jesus. I have been cleansed, purged and accepted in the beloved. For in Christ I live and move and have my being. The blood of Jesus has justified me and has given me access into God's presence.

The power of the Holy Spirit is my comforter, lifting up a standard against all evil visitations and attacks against my life. I am completely set free from the snare of my oppressor. I can boldly declare that the snare is broken and I've escaped, in Jesus name.

PRAYER POINTS

1. Every door in my life open to the enemy, be sealed up by the blood of Jesus.
2. Every evil dedication on my life, be abolished by the blood of Jesus.
3. I receive angelic re-enforcement, to fight and overcome every battle against my life, in Jesus' name.
4. Blood of Jesus, defy the camp of my enemies, in Jesus' name.

5. Every information about my life in the hand of the enemy, be forcefully withdrawn *now*, in Jesus' name.

6. I completely separate my life by the Holy Ghost fire, from every evil on my family line, in Jesus' name.

7. In the name of Jesus, I decree the fire of separation between me and the evil in my environment.

8. I command the strength of the enemy over my life to fail and wither, in Jesus' name.

9. Every evil altar, sacrifice, and idol against my life, thunder fire of God strike them down, in Jesus' name.

10. I command every evil weapon against me to fail and perish, in Jesus' name.

11. Chains and fetters of captivity, break off from my life now, in Jesus' name.

12. Any Satanic agent set up against me, be frustrated and fail, in Jesus' name.

13. All my glory in captivity, be forcefully released now by the thunder fire of God, in Jesus' name.

14. Spirit of the valley in my life, vanish now, in Jesus' name.

15. By the blood of Jesus, I break free from any and every inherited vow of hardship, in Jesus' name.

16. O God, overwhelm my life by the power of your presence, in Jesus' name.

17. Favor of God, envelop my life now, in Jesus' name.

18. Every re-occurrence of evil in my life, be terminated by the Holy Spirit fire, in Jesus' name.

19. O God of Host, order my life into outstanding blessings, in Jesus' name.

20. By the quickening of the Holy Spirit, I overcome every limitation and difficulty, in Jesus' name.

21. The glory of my destiny, shine forth in the strength of the Holy Spirit, in Jesus' name.

22. As the heavens declare the glory of God, O heavens, unfold divine ordained glory in my life, in Jesus' name.
23. My Lord Jesus, the brightness of God's glory, reveal yourself to me.
24. Give thanks to God for answered prayers.

Day Eighteen

TRIUMPHING OVER REPEATED FAILURE AND DEFEAT

Have you prayerfully considered why good things do not come your way easily? You do the same thing many times, over and over again, before getting it right, sometimes never getting through until you are worn out and frustrated. Great achievements are being held back from you because of the pits of failure and defeat, but this prayer session shall without doubt shoot you forward to greatness.

"They reel to and fro, and stagger like a drunken man, And are at their wits' end. Then they cry out to the LORD in their trouble, And He brings them out of their distresses."

(Psalm 107:27–28)

Day Eighteen
TRIUMPHING OVER REPEATED FAILURE AND DEFEAT

PRAISE AND WORSHIP
IT IS WRITTEN

Arise, shine; For your light has come! And the glory of the LORD is risen upon the deep darkness the people; But the LORD will arise over you, and His glory will be seen upon you. The Gentiles shall come to your light, and kings to the brightness of your rising" (Isaiah 60:1–3).

"And I will make you to this people a fortified bronze wall; And they will fight against you, but they shall not prevail against you; For I am with you to save you, and deliver you," says the LORD. "I will deliver you from the hand of the wicked, and I will redeem you from the grip of the terrible" (Jeremiah 15:20–21).

"Do not be a terror to me; You are my hope in the day of doom. Let them be ashamed who persecute me, but do not let me be put to shame; Let them be dismayed, But do not let me be dismayed. Bring on them the day of doom, and destroy them with double destruction!" (Jeremiah 17:17–18).

"For I know the thoughts that I think toward you, says the LORD, thoughts of peace and not of evil, to give you a future and a hope" (Jeremiah 29:11).

"'Therefore all those who devour you shall be devoured; And all your adversaries, every one of them, shall go into captivity; Those who plunder you shall become plunder, and all who prey upon you I will make a prey. For I will restore health to you And heal you of your wounds,' says the LORD, 'Because they called you an outcast saying: "This is Zion; No one seeks her"'" (Jeremiah 30:16–17).

"Your hand shall be lifted against your adversaries, and all your enemies shall be cut off. . . . I will cut off sorceries from your hand, and you shall have no soothsayers" (Micah 5:9, 12).

"Having wiped out the handwriting of requirements that was against us, which was contrary to us. And He has taken it out of the way, having nailed it to the cross. Having disarmed principalities and powers, He made a public spectacle of them, triumphing over them in it" (Colossians 2:14–15).

"Then I heard a loud voice saying in heaven, 'Now salvation, and strength, and the kingdom of our God, and the power of His Christ have come, for the accuser of our brethren, who accused them before our God day and night, has been cast down. And they overcame him by the blood of the Lamb and by the word of their testimony, and they did not love their lives to the death'" (Revelation 12:10–11).

"Rejoice over her, O heaven, and you holy apostles and prophets, for God has avenged you on her!"

Then a mighty angel took up a stone like a great millstone and threw it into the sea, saying, "Thus with violence the great city Babylon shall be thrown down, and shall not be found anymore" (Revelation 18:20–21).

PROPHETIC DECLARATION

"My tongue is the pen of a ready writer" (Psalm 45:1). With a pen of iron, I engrave a decree of desolation upon the heart of the strongman and the stronghold of failure and defeat targeted at me, in Jesus' name. As Jesus declared, "it is finished" (John 19:30) at the cross, so also failure and defeat are finished in my life, in Jesus' name.

PRAYER POINTS

1. You yoke of failure and defeat in my life, be shattered asunder, in Jesus' name.
2. Every cycle of failure and defeat in my life, be broken asunder, in Jesus' name.
3. I reject the fear of failure and defeat in my life, in Jesus' name.
4. Every covenant of failure and defeat in my life, be abolished, in Jesus' name.
5. Every handwriting of failure and defeat on my life, be washed away by the blood of Jesus, in Jesus' name.
6. Every snare of failure on my life, break asunder, in Jesus' name.
7. Let God arise and set me free from the bondage of failure and defeat, in Jesus' name.
8. It is written: "And when the Philistines saw their champion was dead, they fled" (1 Samuel 17:51). O you, my adversaries, your champion, the Devil, has been defeated, I therefore, command you to depart from me and flee, in Jesus' name.
9. Every secret battle bringing defeat into my life, be swallowed up by the Lord God of Host, in Jesus' name.
10. Any area of my life that is open to failure, be delivered by the blood of Jesus, in Jesus' name.
11. By the blood of Jesus, I destroy the root of inherited failure and defeat in my life, in Jesus' name.
12. It is written: "For our God is a consuming fire" (Hebrews 12:29). Therefore, consuming fire of my living God, desolate failure and defeat in my life, in Jesus' name.

13. Every arrow of tragedy set at me, fail and perish, in Jesus' name.

14. Angels of the living God, pull me out from the altars of failure and defeat, in Jesus' name.

15. O arm of God, pull me out from the pit of failure and defeat, in Jesus' name.

16. In the name of Jesus, I break loose from overwhelming clouds of failure and defeat.

17. By the authority that made the heavens and the earth, I establish my dominion over failure and defeat, in Jesus' name.

18. In the name of Jesus, henceforth, let no failure and defeat trouble me, because I am bearing the victorious marks of my Lord Jesus Christ.

19. It is written: "And after that I looked, and, behold, the temple of the tabernacle of the testimony in heaven was opened" (Revelation 15:5, KJV). Therefore, I decree the tabernacle of the heavenly testimony be poured upon my life for multiple miracles, in Jesus' name.

20. In the name of Jesus, I decree failure and defeat upon the strength of my adversaries.

21. O blood of Jesus, minister success and favor into my life, in Jesus' name.

22. Like a rushing mighty wind, precious Holy Spirit, bring forth my miracles and blessings now, in Jesus' name.

23. Unto every defeated area of my life, Holy Spirit confirm victory, in Jesus' name.

24. Give thanks to God for answered prayers.

Day Nineteen
ANGELIC WARFARE

There are numerous blessings awaiting manifestation, held in the spirit realm. There are also some attacks that may be difficult to overcome except you war from the spirit realm. Angelic help would be required to overcome and manifest the blessings. These angels are ever willing and ever ready to assist you. Take advantage of these divine blessings.

"Bless the LORD, you His angels, who excel in strength, who do His word, heeding the voice of His word."

(Psalm 103:20)

Day Nineteen
ANGELIC WARFARE

PRAISE AND WORSHIP
IT IS WRITTEN

The angel of the LORD encamps all around those who fear Him, and delivers them" (Psalm 34:7).

"Let them be like chaff before the wind, and let the angel of the LORD chase them. Let their way be dark and slippery, and let the angel of the LORD pursue them" (Psalm 35:5–6).

"For He shall give His angels charge over you, to keep you in all your ways. In their hands they shall bear you up, lest you dash your foot against a stone" (Psalm 91:11–12).

"Bless the LORD, you His angels, who excel in strength, who do His word, heeding the voice of His word" (Psalm 103:20).

"My God sent His angel and shut the lions' mouths, so that they have not hurt me, because I was found innocent before Him; and also, O king, I have done no wrong before you" (Daniel 6:22).

"But the prince of the kingdom of Persia withstood me twenty-one days; and behold, Michael, one of the chief princes, came to help me, for I had been left alone there with the kings of Persia" (Daniel 10:13).

"Then an angel appeared to Him from heaven, strengthening Him" (Luke 22:43).

"But at night an angel of the Lord opened the prison doors and brought them out" (Acts 5:19).

"Are they not all ministering spirits sent forth to minister for those who will inherit salvation?" (Hebrews 1:14).

PROPHETIC DECLARATION

I come boldly to the throne of grace of the Most High God and ask for an innumerable company of angels to minister to my needs, in Jesus' name. I therefore, welcome the presence of these holy angels to fulfill the divine assignment in my life, as they work and walk with me.

PRAYER POINTS

1. O mighty warrior angels, be girded with strength to fight on my behalf, in Jesus' name.
2. O angels of the Lord, search out the strongholds of my adversaries and pull them down, in Jesus' name.
3. Any warfare against my angels of blessings, be terminated by the blood of Jesus.
4. My angels of blessings under captivity, be released unto me now, in Jesus' name.
5. Angels of the living God, search the realm of the supernatural and bring forth my blessings, in Jesus' name.
6. Protective angels, re-enforce your presence in my life, in Jesus' name.
7. In the name of Jesus, I receive mighty angelic visitations.
8. Angels of divine escape, pull me out from the snare of affliction, in Jesus' name.
9. My appointed angels of destiny, impart the will of God in every area of my life, in Jesus' name.

10. Angels of the living God with your sword drawn out, revisit every defeated battle of my life and give me victory, in Jesus' name.

11. My angels of blessings, overpower every obstacle on your path to bless me, in Jesus' name.

12. Angels of good tidings, minister unto me now, in Jesus' name.

13. My life shall not confuse my angels of blessings, in Jesus' name.

14. Blood of Jesus, attract glorious angels unto me, in Jesus' name.

15. Angels of the living God, search out my stolen blessings and bring them forth, in Jesus' name.

16. Angels of the living God, strike the grave and bring forth my buried glory, in Jesus' name.

17. Worship angels, sing glorious melody into my heart to comfort me, in Jesus' name.

18. Defensive angels, re-enforce your presence in my life, in Jesus' name.

19. Angels assigned to my family line, arise and fulfill your purpose, in Jesus' name.

20. Angels of the living God ascend and descend over my life, in Jesus' name.

21. I receive angelic companions in my journey in life, in Jesus' name.

22. Henceforth, I shall profit in the ministry of angels, in Jesus' name.

23. Healing angels, execute your glorious assignment in my life, in Jesus' name.

24. Give thanks to God for answered prayers.

Day Twenty
THE SIEGE IS OVER

The encompassing problems of your life are to force you to surrender to the enemy of your soul. The re-enforcement of your adversary is to cut off supplies of blessings and favor.

This prayer session, therefore, is to make your encompassing army take flight and make their weapons of non-effect.

"And Moses said to the people, 'Do not be afraid. Stand still, and see the salvation of the LORD, which He will accomplish for you today. For the Egyptians whom you see today, you shall see again no more forever.'"

(Exodus 14:13)

Day Twenty
THE SIEGE IS OVER

PRAISE AND WORSHIP
IT IS WRITTEN

You will also declare a thing, and it will be established for you; So light will shine on your ways. When they cast you down, and you say, 'Exaltation will come!' Then He will save the humble person" (Job 22:28–29).

"As soon as they hear of me they obey me; The foreigners submit to me. The foreigners fade away, and come frightened from their hideouts" (Psalm 18:44–45).

"Though an army may encamp against me, my heart shall not fear; Though war may rise against me, in this I will be confident" (Psalm 27:3).

"Call upon Me in the day of trouble; I will deliver you, and you shall glorify Me" (Psalm 50:15).

"But those who seek my life, to destroy it, Shall go into the lower parts of the earth. They shall fall by the sword; They shall be a portion for jackals" (Psalm 63:9–10).

"All nations surrounded me, but in the name of the LORD I will destroy them. They surrounded me, yes, they surrounded me; But in the name of the LORD I will destroy them. They surrounded me like bees; They were quenched like a fire of thorns; For in the name of the LORD I will destroy them. You pushed me violently, that I might fall, but the LORD helped me. The LORD is my strength and song, And He has become my salvation (Psalm 118:10–14).

"The LORD is righteous; He has cut in pieces the cords of the wicked. Let all those who hate Zion be put to shame and turned back. Let them be as the grass on the housetops, which withers before it grows up" (Psalm 129:4–6).

"'Call to Me, and I will answer you, and show you great and mighty things, which you do not know'" (Jeremiah 33:3).

"For He will finish the work and cut it short in righteousness, because the LORD will make a short work upon the earth" (Romans 9:28).

PROPHETIC DECLARATION

"For the LORD will be your confidence, and will keep your foot from being caught" (Proverbs 3:26).

"By awesome deeds in righteousness You will answer us, O God of our salvation, You who are the confidence of all the ends of the earth, and of the far-off seas" (Psalm 65:5).

I release a royal decree that I shall be abundantly satisfied with the fatness of God's treasure, and God shall make me drink of the river of His pleasures, in Jesus' name. For God has increased me greatly, and made me stronger than my enemies, in Jesus' name (Psalm 36:8–9 and Psalm 105:24).

"As the Lord God of hosts lives and His Spirit lives, I shall not be ashamed, neither shall my face wax pale, in Jesus' name. Because my Redeemer is strong, the Lord of hosts is His name; He shall thoroughly plead my cause, that He may give rest unto me, and disquiet my adversaries. Thus says the Lord God of host unto me, I will deliver you from the hand of the wicked, and I will redeem you from the grip of the terrible" in Jesus' name (Isaiah 29:22; Jeremiah 50:34; Jeremiah 15:21).

As mercy rejoices and triumphs over judgment, so also shall I rejoice and triumph over every condemnation set at me, in Jesus' name.

This declaration comes forth from the Lord of hosts, who is wonderful in counsel, and excellent in working. The siege is indeed over, in Jesus' name.

PRAYER POINTS

1. Blood of Jesus, invade the wicked strongholds hindering the manifestation of my blessings, in Jesus' name.
2. It is written: "All the horns of the wicked also will I cut off; the horns of the righteous shall be exalted" (Psalm 75:10). Therefore, the horns of the wicked lifted up against me, be cut off, in Jesus' name.
3. Jesus, Thou rock of my salvation, strike down evil re-enforcement against my life, in Jesus' name.
4. The troops of darkness against my life, be slain by the Lord God of host, in Jesus' name.
5. The encompassing affliction in my life, be shattered asunder, in Jesus' name.
6. O Lord God of hosts, cut off the supplies of strength of my adversaries, in Jesus' name.
7. I refuse to surrender to affliction, in Jesus' name.
8. I curse the root of siege in my life, in the name of the Lord God of hosts, in Jesus' name.
9. Angel of divine escape, pull me out of every siege, in Jesus' name.
10. Siege stirred up by my parents to afflict me, be quenched, in Jesus' name.
11. O siege, I command you to surrender to Jesus my Lord, in Jesus' name.
12. Every good thing in my life captured by the siege, be reconciled unto me now, by the blood of Jesus.

13. O God, you are the light of my countenance, overwhelm me with favor and glory, in Jesus' name.

14. Every trafficking in the supernatural to cage my spiritman, be shattered, in Jesus' name.

15. O God, You've created me for Your glory, as it is written: "every one who is called by My name: Whom I have created for my glory, I have formed him; yes, I have made him" (Isaiah 43:7). Therefore, glory of God, manifest in my life now, in Jesus' name.

16. My blessing hidden at the uttermost part of the earth, come forth unto me now, in Jesus' name.

17. Anointing of the Holy Spirit, destroy every siege lifted up against me, in Jesus' name.

18. In the name of Jesus, I shall be fruitful, increase abundantly, multiply and become exceedingly mighty in every good thing of life.

19. O Lord God, multiply Your signs, miracles and significant wonders in my life now, in Jesus' name.

20. It is written: "The LORD *is* slow to anger and great in power, And will not at all acquit *the wicked*. The LORD has His way in the whirlwind and in the storm, And the clouds *are* the dust of His feet" (Nahum 1:3). Therefore, I decree whirlwind and storms lifted up against me be quenched, in Jesus' name.

21. Holy Spirit, quicken my life to greatness, in Jesus' name.

22. I proclaim before the heavens and the earth that my siege is over, in Jesus' name.

23. In the name of Jesus, there shall be no reinforcement of siege in my life.

24. Give thanks to God for answered prayers.

Day Twenty-One
HOLY CRY AGAINST EVIL DECREES

God always hears the cry of the afflicted and the oppressed. Make a confident shout of victory against your adversaries and they shall flee in terror; their strongholds shall collapse and you shall possess your possession.

A holy cry is a shout of faith to undo the laws that have held you in bondage. It is a provocation of 'enough is enough' against your taskmaster.

"I cried out to the LORD because of my affliction, and He answered me."

(Jonah 2:2)

Day Twenty-One
HOLY CRY AGAINST EVIL DECREES

PRAISE AND WORSHIP
IT IS WRITTEN

You will also declare a thing, and it will be established for you; So light will shine on your ways" (Job 22:28).

"Hear my cry, O God; Attend to my prayer. From the end of the earth I will cry to You, when my heart is overwhelmed; Lead me to the rock that is higher than I. For You have been a shelter for me, a strong tower from the enemy" (Psalm 61:1–3).

"Let not a slanderer be established in the earth; Let evil hunt the violent man to overthrow him" (Psalm 140:11).

"Woe to those who decree unrighteous decrees, who write misfortune, which they have prescribed . . ." (Isaiah 10:1).

"'For My thoughts are not your thoughts, nor are your ways My ways,' says the LORD. 'For as the heavens are higher than the earth, so are My ways higher than your ways, And My thoughts than your thoughts. For as the rain comes down, and the snow from heaven, and do not return there, but water the earth, and make it bring forth and bud, that it may give seed to the sower and bread to the eater, so shall My word be that goes forth from My mouth; It shall not return to Me void, but it shall accomplish what I please, and it shall prosper in the thing for which I sent it'" (Isaiah 55:8–11),

"Then the LORD said to me, 'You have seen well, for I am ready to perform My word'" (Jeremiah 1:12).

"Therefore thus says the LORD God of hosts: 'Because you speak this word, Behold, I will make My words in your mouth fire, and this people wood, and it shall devour them'" (Jeremiah 5:14).

"'Is not My word like a fire?' says the LORD, 'And like a hammer that breaks the rock in pieces?'" (Jeremiah 23:29).

"For the word of God is living and powerful, and sharper than any two-edged sword, piercing even to the division of soul and spirit, and of joints and marrow, and is a discerner of the thoughts and intents of the heart" (Hebrews 4:12).

PROPHETIC DECLARATION

"And shall God not avenge His own elect who cry out day and night to Him, though He bears long with them?" (Luke 18:7).

Thank you my Heavenly Father, the Creator of heaven and earth, for your ears are open to my cry. The Lord God, "who humbles Himself to behold the things that are in heaven and in the earth" (Psalm 113:6), reach out in Your mercy and deliver me completely from the evil ones, in Jesus' name.

PRAYER POINTS

1. I receive the grace to cry and command divine attention, in Jesus' name.
2. With my heart of faith, I cry unto You, O God, manifest Your signs and wonders in my life, in Jesus' name.
3. I join my voice with the Holy angels to cry unto my Most High King, who answers prayers, in Jesus' name.
4. O Lord my God, remember me for good, in Jesus' name.

5. I lift up my voice to make a resounding shout of victory unto the Most High God for glorious signs and wonders, in Jesus' name.

6. The Lord God who answered the cry of Abraham, Isaac and Jacob, answer me now and favor me indeed, in Jesus' name.

7. The Lord God who answered the cry of Hannah and gave her a child, answer me and bless me, in Jesus' name.

8. The Lord who answered the cry of Jabez and made him honorable, answer me and bless me indeed, in Jesus' name.

9. The Lord who answered the cry of Elijah against the Baal prophets, answer my cry against my persecutors, in Jesus' name.

10. The Lord God who answered the cry of Elisha, manifest Your greatness in my life, in Jesus' name.

11. The Lord God who answered the cry of King Hezekiah, answer me and grant me a peaceful life, in Jesus' name.

12. The Lord God who answered the cry of David against Goliath, answer me and give me victory, in Jesus' name.

13. The Lord God who answered the cry of Daniel in the lions' den, answer me and make me prevail over my enemies, in Jesus' name.

14. The Lord God who answered the cry of Joshua to still the sun and moon, answer my cry and avenge me speedily, in Jesus' name.

15. The Lord God who answered the cry of Paul and Silas to break them free from the bondage of imprisonment, set me free from every trap, in Jesus' name.

16. Lord my God, let my cry reinforce angelic help to war on my behalf, in Jesus' name.

17. Lord my God, let my cry stir up profitable helpers to prosper my destiny, in Jesus' name.

18. Any cry to seal the heavens against me, be silenced by the blood of Jesus, in Jesus' name.

19. Any cry to weary my soul and confuse my spirit, be silenced, in Jesus' name.

20. The cry of the wicked to sabotage my life, be silenced, in Jesus' name.

21. Lord my God, let my cry revive my sleeping glory, in Jesus' name.

22. Henceforth, my cry attracts the favor of God and of men, in Jesus' name.

23. My voice shall be heard among the conquerors and overcomers, in Jesus' name.

24. Give thanks to God for answered prayers.

Day Twenty-Two
QUIETING THE STORMS

Life might not have been favorable to you. It might have stirred up commotion, uproar and confusion of voices. There might have been a sudden change of circumstances affecting you negatively. These storms can be silenced.

Effective praying can change the weather of life to favor you again. Speak against the storms and it shall be still.

"The LORD will fight for you, and you shall hold your peace."

(Exodus 14:14)

Day Twenty-Two
QUIETING THE STORMS

PRAISE AND WORSHIP
IT IS WRITTEN

He dams up the streams from trickling; What is hidden he brings forth to light" (Job 28:11).

"You who still the noise of the seas, the noise of their waves, and the tumult of the peoples" (Psalm 65:7).

"You rule the raging of the sea; When its waves rise, You still them" (Psalm 89:9).

"He calms the storm, so that its waves are still" (Psalm 107:29).

"The nations will rush like the rushing of many waters; But God will rebuke them and they will flee far away, and be chased like the chaff of the mountains before the wind, like a rolling thing before the whirlwind. Then behold, at eventide, trouble! And before the morning, he is no more. This is the portion of those who plunder us, and the lot of those who rob us" (Isaiah 17:13–14).

"For You have been a strength to the poor, a strength to the needy in his distress, a refuge from the storm, a shade from the heat; For the blast of the terrible ones is as a storm against the wall" (Isaiah 25:4).

"But I am the LORD your God, Who divided the sea whose waves roared—the LORD of hosts is His name. And I have put My words in your mouth; I have covered you with the shadow of My hand, that I may plant the heavens, lay the foundations of the earth, And say to Zion, 'You are My people'" (Isaiah 51:15–16).

"They cried there, 'Pharaoh, king of Egypt, is but a noise. He has passed by the appointed time!'" (Jeremiah 46:17).

"Then He arose and rebuked the wind, and said to the sea, 'Peace, be still!' And the wind ceased and there was a great calm. And they feared exceedingly, and said to one another, 'Who can this be, that even the wind and the sea obey Him!'" (Mark 4:39, 41).

PROPHETIC DECLARATION

"The floods have lifted up, O LORD, The floods have lifted up their voice; The floods lift up their waves. The LORD on high is mightier than the noise of many waters, than the mighty waves of the sea" (Psalm 93:3–4).

The Lord my God has broken the jaws of the wicked and plucked the prey out of his teeth. Therefore, as the Lord God of Host lives and as His Spirit lives, I triumph over uproar and commotion, in Jesus' name.

I have been empowered by God Almighty to reign in favor and dignity. God's excellent, majestic and glorious power resides in me. God has also given me dominion over the works of His hand, and subdued my adversaries under me in Jesus' name.

PRAYER POINTS

1. It is written: "casting down arguments and every high thing that exalts itself against the knowledge of God, bringing every thought into captivity to the obedience of Christ" (2 Corinthians 10:5). Therefore, every evil

thought and imagination against my life, be terminated by the blood of Jesus.

2. Blood of Jesus, invade the camp of my adversaries and desolate [annihilate ?] them in Jesus' name.

3. It is written: "How often is the lamp of the wicked put out!" (Job 21:17). Therefore, O lamp of the wicked kindled for my sake, in the name of Jesus be quenched.

4. It is written: "Yea, the light of the wicked shall be put out" (Job 18:5). Therefore, I decree the light of my adversaries be quenched, in Jesus' name.

5. It is written: "And the spark of his fire shall not shine" (Job 18:5 KJV), therefore, O blood of Jesus, extinguish every strange fire stirred up against my life, in Jesus' name.

6. By the blood of Jesus, I decree the source and the strength of affliction in my life perish, in Jesus' name.

7. In the name of Jesus, I command the altars uniting my enemies to arise, scatter, and confuse them.

8. Any authority-strengthening affliction in my life, collapse and perish, in Jesus name.

9. O thou Shekinah throne of the Lord Most High, strike down every throne contending against Your glory in my life, in Jesus' name.

10. It is written: "That the triumphing of the wicked is short, and the joy of the hypocrite but for a moment?" (Job 20:5 KJV). Therefore, O blood of Jesus, stir up Your strength and bring the triumph of the wicked over my life to an end, in Jesus' name.

11. The networking of internal and external storms raging at me, in the name of Jesus, be quenched now.

12. As my Lord Jesus demonstrated His dominion over storms and tempest, in like manner, I decree peace, be still in all areas of my life, in Jesus' name.

13. O flood of adversity stirred up at me, thus says the Lord God of Host, dry up now, in Jesus' name.

14. It is written: "So shall they fear the name of the LORD from the west, and his glory from the rising of the sun. When the enemy shall come in like a flood, the Spirit of the LORD shall lift up a standard against him" (Isaiah 59:19). Therefore, Holy Spirit lift up a standard of desolation against the flooding of my enemies, in Jesus' name.

15. O ye principalities assigned against my life, thus says the Lord God of Host unto thee: "These two things have come to you; Who will be sorry for you? Desolation and destruction, famine and sword. By whom will I comfort you?" (Isaiah 51:19), in Jesus' name.

16. Whatever good thing that the floods and storms have taken away from me, O flooding of the Holy Spirit, restore them unto me now, in Jesus' name.

17. The damage tempests and storms have done to my life, blood of Jesus, repair them now, in Jesus' name.

18. I call for the reinforcement of the Holy Angels to minister deliverance unto me now, in Jesus' name.

19. It is written: "Drop down, ye heavens, from above, and let the skies pour down righteousness: let the earth open, and let them bring forth salvation, and let righteousness spring up together; I the LORD have created it" (Isaiah 45:8 KJV). Therefore, O Lord my God, pour out your blessing upon my life, in Jesus' name.

20. God Most High, who does "great things past finding out, yes, wonders without number" (Job 9:10), overwhelm my life with miraculous blessings, in Jesus' name.

21. It is written: "LORD, You will establish peace for us, for You have also done all our works in us" (Isaiah

26:12). Therefore, Jesus Christ the Prince of Peace, be enthroned in my life, in Jesus' name.

22. Thou tabernacle of testimonies, in the heavens, be stirred up for my sake to bring forth rejoicing and triumphing unto me, in Jesus' name.

23. I consecrate my testimonies unto the blood of Jesus, for unceasing joyful blessings, in Jesus' name.

24. Start giving thanks to God for answered prayers.

Day Twenty-Three
STRONGER THAN THE STRONGMAN

Though your enemies are strong, you are convincingly more powerful than they are. Though they are swift in their evil works, with the strength of God you are mightier than they. They may seem to bring you down, but you shall rise again.

"Because of the covenant I made with you, sealed with blood, I will free your prisoners from death in a waterless dungeon. Come back to the place of safety, all you prisoners, for there is yet hope! I promise this very day that I will repay you two mercies for each of your woes!"

(Zechariah 9:11–12 NLT)

Day Twenty-Three
STRONGER THAN THE STRONGMAN

PRAISE AND WORSHIP
IT IS WRITTEN

For there is no sorcery against Jacob, nor any divination against Israel. It now must be said of Jacob and of Israel, 'Oh, what God has done!'" (Numbers 23:23).

"Say to God, 'How awesome are Your works! Through the greatness of Your power, Your enemies shall submit themselves to You'" (Psalm 66:3).

"O God, how long will the adversary reproach? Will the enemy blaspheme Your name forever? Why do You withdraw Your hand, even Your right hand? Take it out of Your bosom and destroy them. For God is my King from of old, working salvation in the midst of the earth. You divided the sea by Your strength; You broke the heads of the sea serpents in the waters. You broke the heads of Leviathan in pieces, and gave him as food to the people inhabiting the wilderness. You broke open the fountain and the flood; You dried up mighty rivers. The day is Yours, the night also is Yours; You have prepared the light and the sun" (Psalm 74:10–16).

"But if I cast out demons by the Spirit of God, surely the kingdom of God has come upon you. Or how can one enter a strong man's house and plunder his goods, unless he first binds the strong man? And then he will plunder his house" (Matthew 12:28 29).

"And He said to them, 'I saw Satan fall like lightning from heaven. Behold, I give you the authority to trample on serpents and scorpions, and over all the power of the enemy, and nothing shall by any means hurt you'" (Luke 10:18–19).

"But if I cast out demons with the finger of God, surely the kingdom of God has come upon you. When a strong man, fully armed, guards his own palace, his goods are in peace. But when a stronger than he comes upon him and overcomes him, he takes from him all his armor in which he trusted, and divides his spoils" (Luke 11:20–22).

PROPHETIC DECLARATION

"The LORD is a man of war; The LORD is His name" (Exodus 15:3). He is strong and mighty, the LORD mighty in battle (Psalm 24:8). God Almighty has increased me greatly and made me stronger than my enemies (Psalm 105:24). I therefore have dominion over the mighty. (Judges 5:13).

PRAYER POINTS

1. It is written: "Say unto the king and to the queen, humble yourselves, sit down: for your principalities shall come down, even the crown of your glory" (Jeremiah 13:18). Therefore, you the multiple strongmen of darkness set against my life, I subdue you with your strongholds by the blood of Jesus, in Jesus' name.

2. It is written: "They fought from heaven; the stars in their courses fought against Sisera" (Judges 5:20). Therefore, every battle in the heavenlies against my life, by the blasting of the blood of Jesus, become an empty waste, in Jesus' name.

3. Thus says the Lord of Host unto all my adversaries, you shall be wearied on your high places and shall not prevail against me, in Jesus' name.

4. My Lord Jesus, Thou Lion of the tribe of Judah, devour every trap and captivity set for my life, in Jesus' name.

5. It is written: "Let not a slanderer be established in the earth; Let evil hunt the violent man to overthrow him" (Psalm 140:11). Therefore, no evil word, thoughts or imagination shall come to pass in my life, in Jesus' name.

6. Every wicked priest hired against my life, hear your divine judgment, "The calamity of Moab is near at hand, And his affliction comes quickly" (Jeremiah 48:16), in Jesus' name.

7. It is written: "A fire goes before Him, and burns up His enemies round about" (Psalm 97:3). Therefore, let the fire of your wrath consume all opposition to my greatness, in Jesus' name.

8. It is written: "For the LORD of hosts has purposed, and who will annul it? His hand is stretched out, and who will turn it back?" (Isaiah 14:27). Henceforth, in the name of Jesus, abundant favor shall be my lot.

9. It is written: "Your throne is established from of old; You are from everlasting" (Psalm 93:2). I therefore lift high Your Shekinah throne, O MOST High God, reign in Your fullness in my life, in Jesus' name.

10. Thus says the Lord God of Host to my adversaries, "For the Lord has poured out on you the spirit of deep sleep, and has closed your eyes" (Isaiah 29:10), in Jesus' name.

11. "You will be punished by the LORD of hosts with thunder and earthquake and great noise, with storm and tempest and the flame of devouring fire" (Isaiah 29:6). Therefore, O Lord God of Host, visit the strongholds of my adversaries with thunder, earthquake, great noise, storm, tempest and flame of devouring fire, in Jesus' name.

12. It is written: "For the terrible one is brought to nothing, the scornful one is consumed" (Isaiah 29:20). Therefore, O you the terrible, set against me, be brought to naught, in Jesus' name.

13. In the name of Jesus, I shall not be ashamed; neither shall my face wax pale (Isaiah 29:22).

14. It is written: "The heavens declare his righteousness, and all the people see His glory" (Psalm 97:6). Therefore, O heavens declare now my glory, in Jesus' name.

15. It is written: "He raises the poor from the dust and lifts the beggar from the ash heap, to set them among princes and make them inherit the throne of glory. For the pillars of the earth are the LORD's, And He has set the world upon them" (1 Samuel 2:8). Therefore, O Lord God, raise me and lift me up to my divine positioning, in Jesus' name.

16. By the authority in the blood of Jesus, I inherit my throne of glory, in Jesus' name.

17. Blood of Jesus, anoint my life with an excellent spirit, in Jesus' name.

18. By the ordinances that made the heavens and earth, I prevail over the mighty, in Jesus' name.

19. In the name of Jesus, I decree the spoiler to devour the weapons and the strength of my adversaries.

20. The fierceness of Leviathan targeted at me, turn back and strike down your stronghold, in Jesus' name.

21. In the name of Jesus, I overcome and overpower the strongman assigned against my life.

22. Every blessing due to me captured by the strongman, I possess you by the blood of Jesus.

23. In the name of Jesus, I refuse to be spoiled by the strongman.

24. Give thanks to God for answered prayers.

Day Twenty-Four
PROPHETIC WARFARE

"For we do not wrestle against flesh and blood, but against principalities, against powers, against the rulers of the darkness of this age, against spiritual hosts of wickedness in the heavenly places."

(Ephesians 6:12)

Life is full of conflicting, opposing issues. So many people are troubled on every side, tormented internally and overwhelmed with fear. But it is absolutely possible to walk in victory. Make a prophetic proclamation and see the salvation of the Lord.

Day Twenty-Four
PROPHETIC WARFARE

PRAISE AND WORSHIP
IT IS WRITTEN

H e teacheth [God teaches] my hands to war, so that a bow of steel is broken by mine arms" (Psalm 18:34).

"The LORD shall go forth like a mighty man; He shall stir up His zeal like a man of war. He shall cry out, yes, shout aloud; He shall prevail against His enemies. I have held my peace a long time, I have been still and restrained myself. Now I will cry like a woman in labor, I will pant and gasp at once" (Isaiah 42:13–14).

"No man shall be able to stand before you all the days of your life; as I was with Moses, so I will be with you. I will not leave you nor forsake you" (Joshua 1:5).

Let God arise, and let my enemies be scattered; let them also that hate me flee before me. As smoke is driven away, so drive them away; as wax melts before the fire, so let the wicked perish at the presence of God (Psalm 68:1–2).

"The LORD will cause your enemies who rise against you to be defeated before your face; they shall come out against you one way and flee before you seven ways" (Deuteronomy 28:7).

"The eternal God is your refuge, and underneath are the everlasting arms; He will thrust out the enemy from before you, and will say, 'Destroy!'" (Deuteronomy 33:27).

"Your sandals shall be iron and bronze; As your days, so shall your strength be" (Deuteronomy 33:25).

"Your enemies shall submit to you, and you shall tread down their high places" (Deuteronomy 33.29).

"Who frustrates the signs of the babblers, and drives diviners mad; Who turns wise men backward, and makes their knowledge foolishness" (Isaiah 44:25).

"He frustrates the devices of the crafty, so that their hands cannot carry out their plans" (Job 5:12).

"But the LORD your God will deliver them over to you, and will inflict defeat upon them until they are destroyed" (Deuteronomy 7:23).

"Those who hate you will be clothed with shame, and the dwelling place of the wicked will come to nothing" (Job 8:22).

"Be shattered, O you peoples, and be broken in pieces! Give ear, all you from far countries. Gird yourselves, but be broken in pieces; Gird yourselves, but be broken in pieces. Take counsel together, but it will come to nothing; Speak the word, but it will not stand, for God is with us" (Isaiah 8:9–10).

"The LORD brings the counsel of the nations to nothing; He makes the plans of the peoples of no effect" (Psalm 33:10).

"Their sword shall enter their own heart, and their bows shall be broken" (Psalm 37:15).

"I will say of the LORD, 'He is my refuge and my fortress; my God, in Him I will trust. . . . You shall not be afraid of the terror by night, nor of the arrow that flies by day, nor of the pestilence that walks in darkness, nor of the destruction that lays waste at noonday. A thousand may fall at your side, and ten thousand at your right hand; But it shall not come near you'" (Psalm 91:2; 5–7).

"I have set the LORD always before me; Because he is at my right hand, I shall not be moved" (Psalm 16:8).

"For the scepter of wickedness shall not rest on the land allotted to the righteous, lest the righteous reach out their hands to iniquity" (Psalm 125:3).

"For by thee O Lord, I have run through a troop; And by my God have I leaped over a wall" (Psalm 18:29, KJV).

"Arise, O LORD; Save me, O my God! For You have struck all my enemies on the cheekbone; You have broken the teeth of the ungodly" (Psalm 3:7).

"Upon the wicked He will rain coals; Fire and brimstone and a burning wind shall be the portion of their cup" (Psalm 11:6).

"He sent out His arrows and scattered the foe, lightnings in abundance, and He vanquished them" (Psalm 18:14).

"Evil shall slay the wicked, and those who hate the righteous shall be condemned" (Psalm 34:21).

"'The pride of your heart has deceived you, you who dwell in the clefts of the rock, whose habitation is high; You who say in your heart, "Who will bring me down to the ground?" Though you ascend as high as the eagle, and though you set your nest among the stars, from there I will bring you down,' says the LORD" (Obadiah 1:3–4).

"Therefore God also has highly exalted Him and given Him the name which is above every name, that at the name of Jesus every knee should bow, of those in heaven, and of those on earth, and of those under the earth, and that every tongue should confess that Jesus Christ is Lord, to the glory of God the Father" (Philippians 2:9–11).

"For by Him all things were created that are in heaven and that are on earth, visible and invisible, whether thrones or dominions or principalities or powers. All things were created through Him and for Him. And He is before all things, and in Him all things consist" (Colossians 1:16–17).

"He who leads into captivity shall go into captivity; he who kills with the sword must be killed with the sword. Here is the patience and the faith of the saints" (Revelation 13:10).

Any evil set against me, "thus says the Lord God: It shall not stand, nor shall it come to pass" (Isaiah 7:7), in Jesus' name.

"In the beginning was the Word, and the Word was with God, and the Word was God. He was in the beginning with God. All things were made through Him, and without Him nothing was made that was made. In Him was life, and the life was the light of men. And the light shines in the darkness, and the darkness did not comprehend it" (John. 1:1–5).

"Look, a people rises like a lioness, and lifts itself up like a lion; It shall not lie down until it devours the prey, And drinks the blood of the slain" (Numbers 23:24).

"Why do the nations rage, and the people plot a vain thing? The kings of the earth set themselves, and the rulers take counsel together, against the LORD and against His Anointed, saying 'Let us break their bonds in pieces And cast away their cords from us.' He who sits in the heavens shall laugh; The Lord shall hold them in derision. Then He shall speak to them in His wrath, and distress them in His deep displeasure" (Psalm 2:1–5).

PROPHETIC DECLARATION:

I have received grace to fight opposing forces to the Kingdom of God and overcome. Jesus, "the Lord strong and mighty, the Lord mighty in battle" (Psalm 24:8) has the absolute right and power to reign in my life.

PRAYER POINTS

1. Jehovah Elohim, my Eternal Creator, create wonderful miracles in my life, in Jesus' name.
2. Adonai-Jehovah, the Sovereign Lord, establish the supremacy of your power over my life, in Jesus' name.

3. Jehovah-Jireh, the Lord will see and provide, meet all my needs according to your riches in glory by Christ Jesus.

4. Jehovah-Nissi, the Lord our banner, defend my destiny and give me resounding victory, in Jesus' name.

5. Jehovah-Ropheka, the Lord our healer, give me perfect health, in Jesus' name.

6. Jehovah-Shalom, the Lord our peace, make me dwell in peace and rejoicing, in Jesus' name.

7. Jehovah-Tsidkeenu, the Lord our righteousness, grant me grace to walk worthy of You, in Jesus' name.

8. Jehovah-MekaddishKem, the Lord our Sanctifier, sanctify my body, soul, and spirit, in Jesus' name.

9. Jehovah-Saboath, the Lord of hosts, fight my battles and give me victory, in Jesus' name.

10. Jehovah-Shammah, the Lord is present, manifest your greatness in every area of my life, in Jesus' name.

11. Jehovah-Elyon, the Lord Most High, bless me indeed, in Jesus' name.

12. Jehovah-Rohi, the Lord my Shepherd, guide me to miraculous victories, in Jesus' name.

13. Jehovah-Hoseenu, the Lord our Maker, make me the head, and not the tail, in Jesus' name.

14. Jehovah Elohay, the Lord my God, exalt me with favor, in Jesus' name.

15. El-Shaddai, God Almighty, empower me for signs and wonders, in Jesus' name.

16. The Lord my Rock, smite asunder the pursuit of my adversaries, in Jesus' name.

17. Warfare of thoughts against my life shall not prosper, in Jesus' name.

18. Through the blood of Jesus, I subdue wicked authorities and dominion set against my life, in Jesus' name.

19. In Jesus' name, I decree the strength of fierce attacks against my life to wither.

20. Blood of Jesus, quench all the flaming missiles of the wicked targeted at me, in Jesus' name.

21. I draw strength from the throne of grace to overcome every backlashing of the wicked, in Jesus' name.

22. Blood of Jesus, abolish every strategy and deceit of the wicked ones against my life, in Jesus' name.

23. Every monitoring device of the wicked ones against my life, be shattered asunder, in Jesus' name.

24. Give thanks to God for answered prayers.

Day Twenty-Five
LET GOD ARISE!

This is a prayer from a desperate heart, who requires immediate divine intervention. It is for someone coming out of a barren life to fruitful living. Someone will rise out of worthless inferior living to abundant, glorious living. Pray with expectation and radiate the glory of God Almighty.

"For Zion's sake I will not hold My peace, And for Jerusalem's sake I will not rest, Until her righteousness goes forth as brightness, and her salvation as a lamp that burns."

(Isaiah 62:1)

Day Twenty-Five
LET GOD ARISE

PRAISE AND WORSHIP
IT IS WRITTEN

"Look, a people rises like a lioness, and lifts itself up like a lion; It shall not lie down until it devours the prey, and drinks the blood of the slain" (Numbers 23:24).

"He made him ride in the heights of the earth, that he might eat the produce of the fields; He made him draw honey from the rock, and oil from the flinty rock" (Deuteronomy 32:13).

"There is no one like the God of Jeshurun, Who rides the heavens to help you, and in His Excellency on the clouds" (Deuteronomy 33:26).

"Arise, shine; for your light has come! And the glory of the LORD is risen upon you. For behold, the darkness shall cover the earth, and deep darkness the people; But the LORD will arise over you, and His glory will be seen upon you. The Gentiles shall come to your light, and kings to the brightness of your rising" (Isaiah 60:1–3).

"To console those who mourn in Zion, to give them beauty for ashes, the oil of joy for mourning, the garment of praise for the spirit of heaviness; That they may be called trees of righteousness, the planting of the LORD, that He may be glorified" (Isaiah 61:3).

"Will a lion roar in the forest, when he has no prey? Will a young lion cry out of his den, if he has caught nothing?" (Amos 3:4).

"He rains ruin upon the strong, so that fury comes upon the fortress" (Amos 5:9).

"For I am the LORD, I do not change; Therefore you are not consumed, O sons of Jacob" (Malachi 3:6).

"And shall God not avenge His own elect who cry out day and night to Him, though He bears long with them?" (Luke 18:7).

PROPHETIC DECLARATION

O Lord my God, You're my strength. It's time for You to arise and help, rescue and prosper my life. The brightness of God's glory has arisen upon me. The strength of the Almighty has given me victory.

PRAYER POINTS

1. Holy Spirit, empower my words to desolate the attackers of my destiny, in Jesus' name.
2. It is written: "And a mighty angel took up a stone like a great millstone, and cast it into the sea, saying, thus with violence shall that great city Babylon be thrown down, and shall be found no more at all" (Revelation 18:21 KJV). Therefore, thou mighty angel of God, like a great millstone cast the strongholds of my adversaries into the sea of desolation, in Jesus' name.
3. The stronghold of darkness on assignment against my life be thrown down and be found no more at all, in Jesus' name.
4. It is written: "behold, I lay in Zion a stumbling stone and rock of offense" (Romans 9:33 KJV) Therefore,

thou rock of offense tear down the defenses of my oppressors, in Jesus' name.

5. It is written: "And whosoever shall fall on this stone shall be broken: but on whomsoever it shall fall, it will grind him to powder" (Matthew 21:44 KJV). Therefore, Jesus Christ my Rock of Ages, collide with all my adversaries, in Jesus' name.

6. It is written: "A stone was cut out without hands, which smote the image" (Daniel 2:34 KJV). Therefore, thou smiting stone of destruction, crush the dominion of darkness over my life, in Jesus' name.

7. Like a tempest of hail and like a destroying storm, I scatter every wicked gathering against my life, in Jesus' name.

8. It is written: "Behold, with a great plague will the Lord smite" (2 Chronicles 21:14). Therefore, O Lord God of Host, smite the altars, thrones and shrines set against my life with great plagues, in Jesus' name.

9. O ye attackers of my destiny, "I call heaven and earth to record this day against you" (Deuteronomy 30:19 KJV), in Jesus' name.

10. In the name of Jesus, I call for the great innumerable armies of angels to war on my behalf and bring forth victory unto me.

11. Stir up your wrath and your indignation, O God, against the violent pursuit of my enemies, in Jesus' name.

12. Let God arise to perfect every good thing that concerns me, in Jesus' name.

13. Angels of the living God, spoil the camp of my enemies and restore blessings unto me, in Jesus' name.

14. It is written: "He makes wars cease to the end of the earth; He breaks the bow and cuts the spear in two; He burns the chariot in the fire" (Psalm 46:9). Jehovah my

sovereign God, bring wars to an end in my life, in Jesus' name.

15. It is written: "And the God of peace shall crush Satan under your feet" (Romans 16:20). Therefore, O God of peace, establish peace in all areas of my life, in Jesus' name.

16. It is written: "The voice of rejoicing and salvation is in the tabernacles of the righteous" (Psalm 118:15 KJV). Therefore, rejoicing and triumphing shall never cease in my life, in Jesus' name.

17. Jesus, the lion of the tribe of Judah, devour every affliction in my life, in Jesus' name.

18. I decree to my soul, awake and be strengthened with might for victory, in Jesus' name.

19. Awake my spirit man, in the brightness of God's glory, in Jesus' name.

20. Every dead situation in my life, awake unto glory, in Jesus' name.

21. My falling glory, arise, in Jesus' name.

22. My buried glory, come alive, in Jesus' name.

23. My divine ordained glory, manifest now, in Jesus' name.

24. Give thanks to God for answered prayer.

Day Twenty-Six
I SHALL SURELY OVERCOME

Victory is inevitable. Your success is certain. Without any doubt, your destiny is secured in the Lord Jesus. I see God rewarding the difficulties of your past with joy and success. Pray until the joy of victory overwhelms your soul.

"The LORD of hosts is with us; The God of Jacob is our refuge."

(Psalm 46:7)

Day Twenty-Six
I SHALL SURELY OVERCOME

PRAISE AND WORSHIP
IT IS WRITTEN

"The LORD will fight for you, and you shall hold your peace" (Exodus 14:14).

"For the LORD of hosts has purposed, and who will annul it? His hand is stretched out, and who will turn it back?" (Isaiah 14:27).

"Fear not, for I am with you; be not dismayed, for I am your God. I will strengthen you, yes, I will help you, I will uphold you with My righteous right hand. Behold, all those who were incensed against you shall be ashamed and disgraced; They shall be as nothing, and those who strive with you shall perish. You shall seek them and not find them—those who contended with you. Those who war against you shall be as nothing, as a nonexistent thing" (Isaiah 41:10–12).

"The LORD shall go forth like a mighty man; He shall stir up His zeal like a man of war. He shall cry out, yes, shout aloud; He shall prevail against His enemies. I have held My peace a long time, I have been still and restrained Myself. Now I will cry like a woman in labor, I will pant and gasp at once. I will lay waste the mountains and hills, And dry up all their vegetation;

I will make the rivers coastlands, And I will dry up the pools. I will bring the blind by a way they did not know; I will lead them in paths they have not known. I will make darkness light before them, and crooked places straight. These things I will do for them, and not forsake them" (Isaiah 42:13–16).

"Who frustrates the signs of the babblers, And drives diviners mad; Who turns wise men backward, and makes their knowledge foolishness; Who confirms the word of His servant, and performs the counsel of His messengers; Who says to Jerusalem, 'You shall be inhabited,' To the cities of Judah, 'You shall be built,' and I will raise up her waste places" (Isaiah 44:25–26).

"I will go before you and make the crooked places straight; I will break in pieces the gates of bronze, and cut the bars of iron. I will give you the treasures of darkness and hidden riches of secret places, that you may know that I, the LORD, Who calls you by your name, am the God of Israel" (Isaiah 45:2–3).

"And I will make you to this people a fortified bronze wall; And they will fight against you, but they shall not prevail against you; For I am with you to save you and deliver you," says the LORD. "I will deliver you from the hand of the wicked, and I will redeem you from the grip of the terrible" (Jeremiah 15:20–21).

"Ah, Lord GOD! Behold, You have made the heavens and the earth by Your great power and outstretched arm. There is nothing too hard for You . . . Behold, I am the LORD, the God of all flesh. Is there anything too hard for Me?" (Jeremiah 32:17, 27).

Then I heard a loud voice saying in heaven, "Now salvation, and strength, and the kingdom of our God, and the power of His Christ have come, for the accuser of our brethren, who accused them before our God day and night, has been cast down" (Revelation 12:10).

PROPHETIC DECLARATION

Thus says the LORD God of Host to all my adversaries, you shall be wearied on the high places and shall not prevail against me.

"Awake, awake, put on strength, O arm of the LORD! Awake as in the ancient days, in the generations of old. Are You not the arm that cut Rahab apart, and wounded the serpent? Are You not the One who dried up the sea, the waters of the great deep; That made the depths of the sea a road For the redeemed to cross over? (Isaiah 51:9–10).

Therefore, arise for my sake O arm of God and fight my battles and give me victory, in Jesus' name. You are the Lord God who teaches me to profit, who leads me by the way that I should go, arise and fulfill your glorious pleasure in my life, in Jesus' name. It is written: "My counsel will stand and I will do all my pleasure" (Isaiah 46:10).

Therefore, my soul magnifies the Lord Most High, the Holy One of Israel for He has done excellent things known in all the heavens and on the earth. The Lord God has made the earth by His power; He has established the world by His wisdom, and has stretched out the heavens by His understanding. When God utters His voice, there is a multitude of waters in the heavens. "For his molded image is falsehood, and there is no breath in them. They are futile, a work of errors; In the time of their punishment they shall perish" (Jeremiah 51:15–18), in Jesus' name.

PRAYER POINTS

1. Thou wicked throne set against my life, be dashed into pieces, in Jesus' name.
2. Thou throne of the wicked, suppressing my glory, be shattered, in Jesus name.
3. Thus saith the LORD God of Host to the principalities attached to my life, "You will be punished by the

LORD of hosts with thunder and earthquake and great noise, with storm and tempest and the flame of devouring fire" (Isaiah 29:6), in Jesus' name.

4. In the name of Jesus, I proclaim desolation against the defended cities of my adversaries.

5. You multitude of wicked thoughts and imaginations against my life, become an empty waste, in Jesus' name.

6. I decree the habitation of my oppressors be forsaken and left like a wilderness, in Jesus' name.

7. O you re-enforcement of the wicked against my life, hear the Word of God, "These two things have come to you; Who will be sorry for you?—Desolation and destruction, famine and sword—by whom will I comfort you?" (Isaiah 51:19), in Jesus' name.

8. The boasting crown of my oppressors, shatter, in Jesus' name.

9. Thou fist of wickedness set against my life, dry up now, in Jesus' name.

10. Thou raging of enemies, your horns are cut off and your arms broken asunder, in Jesus' name.

11. Every wicked priest hired against my life hear your divine judgment, your calamity is near at hand, And your affliction comes quickly in Jesus' name (Jeremiah 48:16).

12. In the name of Jesus, I decree spoilers to devour the strength of the strongman set against me.

13. Every vow to afflict my life, receive perpetual shame, which shall not be forgotten, in Jesus' name.

14. O you my oppressors, become an object of ridicule and disgrace, in Jesus' name.

15. You gates of my adversaries, crumble, in Jesus' name.

16. Strength to overcome, be renewed in my life, in Jesus' name.

17. Heavens of my miracles open now, in Jesus' name.
18. Angels of my miracles, triumph over all adversaries and unfold my miracles unto me now, in Jesus' name.
19. Blood of Jesus, reconcile me now to my miracles, in Jesus' name.
20. Holy Spirit, quicken my life to encounter divine presence now, in Jesus' name.
21. Henceforth, the zeal of the Lord of Host shall perform glorious signs and wonders in my life, in Jesus' name.
22. In any area of my life where I've been defeated, I claim back my victory now, in Jesus' name.
23. The mantle to overcome all opposition manifests now, in my life, in Jesus' name.
24. Give thanks to God for answered prayers.

Day Twenty-Seven

REIGNING IN LIFE
AS KING

It is time for your godly influence to increase. The sovereign Lord rules over all and He reigns in you. Exercise your dominion and prevail over all opposition.

"Behold, a king will reign in righteousness, and princes will rule with justice."

(Isaiah 32:1)

Day Twenty-Seven
REIGNING IN LIFE
AS KING

PRAISE AND WORSHIP
IT IS WRITTEN

The LORD said to my Lord, 'Sit at My right hand, till I make Your enemies Your footstool.' The LORD shall send the rod of Your strength out of Zion. Rule in the midst of Your enemies!" (Psalm 110:1–2).

"He raises the poor out of the dust, and lifts the needy out of the ash heap, that He may seat him with princes—with the princes of His people" (Psalm 113:7–8).

"When the LORD brought back the captivity of Zion, We were like those who dream. Then our mouth was filled with laughter, and our tongue with singing. Then they said among the nations, 'The LORD has done great things for them.' The LORD has done great things for us, and we are glad" (Psalm 126:1–3).

"And raised us up together, and made us sit together in the heavenly places in Christ Jesus" (Ephesians 2:6).

"For by grace you have been saved through faith, and that not of yourselves; it is the gift of God, not of works, lest anyone should boast. For we are His workmanship, created in Christ

Jesus for good works, which God prepared beforehand that we should walk in them" (Ephesians 2:8–10).

"To the intent that now the manifold wisdom of God might be made known by the church to the principalities and powers in the heavenly places" (Ephesians 3:10).

"But you are a chosen generation, a royal priesthood, a holy nation, His own special people, that you may proclaim the praises of Him who called you out of darkness into His marvelous light" (1 Peter 2:9)

"And has made us kings and priests to His God and Father, to Him be glory and dominion forever and ever. Amen" (Revelation 1:6).

"And have made us kings and priests to our God; and we shall reign on the earth" (Revelation 5:10)

PROPHETIC DECLARATION

I am God's own purchased special individual. The immeasurable, unlimited and surpassing greatness of God's power dwells in me. I have the power, authority, privilege and right to divine treasure. Through the grace of God, I belong to the royal race and because Jesus reigns, I shall reign also.

PRAYER POINTS

1. O God, forgive me of being ignorant of my position in Christ, in Jesus' name.

2. Through the blood of Jesus, I rediscover my identity in Christ.

3. I rededicate my life to Jesus and the power of His blood, in Jesus' name.

4. O Lord God, adorn me with the robe of honor and the scepter of power, in Jesus' name.

5. I put on my priestly robe to minister unto the Lord God Almighty, in Jesus' name.

6. I put on my kingly crown to exercise my dominion in Christ Jesus.
7. O mantle of greatness and favor, fall on me, in Jesus' name.
8. O Lord God, increase my godly influence, in Jesus' name.
9. In the name of Jesus, I prevail over every obstacle to greatness.
10. Through the resurrection power of my Lord Jesus, I am at a superior height to manifest God's glory, in Jesus' name.
11. I am born to reign in peace, and joy in the Holy Spirit, in Jesus' name.
12. I have been raised to be more than a conqueror, in Jesus' name.
13. Henceforth, evil shall not have dominion over me, in Jesus' name.
14. Holy Spirit, quicken accelerated blessings in all areas of my life, in Jesus' name.
15. The Lord my God is the lifter up of my head, therefore, O Lord my God exalt my head with honor, in Jesus' name.
16. Anointing to rule in glory and favor rest upon me now, in Jesus' name.
17. O Lord, confirm your power in my weaknesses, in Jesus' name.
18. O Lord my God, give me the heart of a ruler and not that of a slave, in Jesus' name.
19. Let self decrease and Jesus grow prominently in my life, in Jesus' name.
20. I gloriously step into great accomplishments for the kingdom of God, in Jesus' name.
21. I speak as God's oracle that it shall be well with me, in Jesus' name.

22. O brightness of my glory, shine forth, in Jesus' name.
23. My heart is filled with joy and my mouth with praise for uncommon blessings, in Jesus' name.
24. Give thanks to God for answered prayers.

Day Twenty-Eight

LIVING IN DOMINION

You have been divinely put in a prestigious position. You are destined to make a godly impact. You have power to rule and enjoy life. Rise up to your responsibilities and shine!

"You have made him to have dominion over the works of Your hands; You have put all things under his feet."

(Psalm 8:6)

Day Twenty-Eight
LIVING IN DOMINION

PRAISE AND WORSHIP
IT IS WRITTEN

Give us help from trouble, for the help of man is useless. Through God we will do valiantly, for it is He who shall tread down our enemies" (Psalm 108:12–13).

"Shall the prey be taken from the mighty, or the captives of the righteous be delivered? But thus says the LORD: 'Even the captives of the mighty shall be taken away, and the prey of the terrible be delivered; For I will contend with him who contends with you, and I will save your children. I will feed those who oppress you with their own flesh, and they shall be drunk with their own blood as with sweet wine. All flesh shall know that I, the LORD, am your Savior, And your Redeemer, the Mighty One of Jacob'" (Isaiah 49:24–26).

"For the Lord GOD will help me; Therefore I will not be disgraced; Therefore I have set my face like a flint, and I know that I will not be ashamed. He is near who justifies me; Who will contend with me? Let us stand together. Who is my adversary? Let him come near Me. Surely the Lord GOD will help Me; Who is he who will condemn me? Indeed they will all grow old like a garment; The moth will eat them up" (Isaiah 50:7–9).

"In righteousness you shall be established; You shall be far from oppression, for you shall not fear; And from terror, for it shall not come near you. Indeed they shall surely assemble, but not because of Me. Whoever assembles against you shall fall for your sake. 'Behold, I have created the blacksmith who blows the coals in the fire, who brings forth an instrument for his work; And I have created the spoiler to destroy. No weapon formed against you shall prosper, and every tongue which rises against you in judgment You shall condemn. This is the heritage of the servants of the LORD, and their righteousness is from Me,' Says the LORD" (Isaiah 54:14–17).

"'They will fight against you, but they shall not prevail against you. For I am with you,' says the LORD, 'to deliver you'" (Jeremiah 1:19).

"Let them be ashamed who persecute me, but do not let me be put to shame; Let them be dismayed, but do not let me be dismayed. Bring on them the day of doom, and destroy them with double destruction!" (Jeremiah 17:18).

"He did not waver at the promise of God through unbelief, but was strengthened in faith, giving glory to God, and being fully convinced that what He had promised He was also able to perform" (Romans 4:20–21).

"And the Lord will deliver me from every evil work and preserve me for His heavenly kingdom. To Him be glory forever and ever. Amen!" (2 Timothy 4:18).

PROPHETIC DECLARATION

I have been endued with an exceeding great power of the Holy Spirit. I have an eternal glorious power of the Most High God dwelling in me. The conquering power that brought the world of darkness to shame is upon me. My God Jehovah has given me dominion over all the works of His hand (Psalm 8:6). Therefore, I subdue every opposition to my miracles, signs and glorious wonders, in Jesus' name.

PRAYER POINTS

1. Blood of Jesus, cleanse, purge and sanctify my life, in Jesus' name.
2. Any evil authority over my life, perish, in Jesus' name.
3. By the blood of Jesus, I command every evil trafficking in my environment to come under the arrest of the Holy Spirit, in Jesus' name.
4. Holy Spirit release strength to every weak area of my life, in Jesus' name.
6. Every hidden bondage in my life, break asunder and vanish unto desolation, in Jesus' name.
5. Every leakage in the vessel of my life, be sealed by the blood of Jesus and be fortified by the Holy Spirit fire, in Jesus' name.
7. In Jesus' name, I command that the secret strength of my adversaries be exposed and be disgraced, in Jesus' name.
8. Every renewal of Satanic strategy in my life become an empty waste, in Jesus' name.
9. The mantle of confidence of my adversaries, be torn off and be burnt, in Jesus' name.
10. It is written: "That the man of the earth may no more oppress" (Psalm 10:18 KJV). Therefore, I decree the oppression of the wicked over my life to perish, in Jesus' name.
11. O my enemies, thus saith the Lord God of Host unto you, your destruction will come to a perpetual end therefore, be subdued by terror, in Jesus' name.
12. My Lord Jesus has made me to have dominion over the works of His hands; and has put all things under my feet (Psalm 8:6). Therefore, I subdue thrones, powers and principalities under my feet and I rule over them, in Jesus' name.

13. It is written: "Break the arm of the wicked and the evil man; Seek out his wickedness until You find none" (Psalm 10:15). Therefore, I decree the arm of the wicked over my life, be broken asunder, in Jesus' name.

14. It is written: "O GOD the Lord, the strength of my salvation, You have covered my head in the day of battle" (Psalm 140:7). O Lord God, protect me from the fury of my enemies, in Jesus' name.

15. It is written: "In Your mercy cut off my enemies, and destroy all those who afflict my soul; For I am Your servant" (Psalm 143:12). O Lord God, cut off my enemies and destroy all them that afflict my soul, in Jesus' name.

16. It is written: "Who executes justice for the oppressed, Who gives food to the hungry. The LORD gives freedom to the prisoners" (Psalm 146:7). Therefore, let the power that raised Jesus from death release all my blessings from the prisons of the wicked, in Jesus' name.

17. All my blessings that have been strangely transferred, hear ye the voice of your Creator, manifest now, in my life, in Jesus' name.

18. I decree my life to start manifesting the glory and power of the living God, in Jesus' name.

19. It is written: "Greater is he that is in you, than he that is in the world" (1 John 4:4, kjv). Therefore, the champion in me, manifest now, in Jesus' name.

20. The mantle of the Highest is upon me, henceforth, I live in perpetual dominion, in Jesus' name.

21. I decree before the heavens and let the earth witness these declarations, that I am a perpetual overcomer, in Jesus' name.

22. The anointing of greatness is upon my life, therefore I shall be great and exceedingly great, in Jesus' name.

23. Dominion anointing break forth in my life now, in Jesus' name.
24. Thank God for answered prayer, in Jesus' name.

Day Twenty-Nine
PROPHETIC HEALING

It is God's intent to heal you. Healing is for God's children—it is the children's bread. Your health can be restored; it does not matter how degenerated your life situation is. The miracle of healing is yours as you call on God.

"Heal me, O LORD, and I shall be healed; Save me, and I shall be saved, for You are my praise."

(Jeremiah 17:14)

Day Twenty-Nine
PROPHETIC HEALING

PRAISE AND WORSHIP
IT IS WRITTEN

And the LORD will take away from you all sickness, and will afflict you with none of the terrible diseases of Egypt which you have known, but will lay them on all those who hate you" (Deuteronomy 7:15).

"Many are the afflictions of the righteous, but the LORD delivers him out of them all. He guards all his bones; Not one of them is broken" (Psalm 34:19–20).

"Bless the LORD, O my soul; And all that is within me, bless His holy name! Bless the LORD, O my soul, and forget not all His benefits: Who forgives all your iniquities, Who heals all your diseases, Who redeems your life from destruction, Who crowns you with loving-kindness and tender mercies, Who satisfies your mouth with good things, so that your youth is renewed like the eagle's" (Psalm 103:1–5).

"He sent His word and healed them, and delivered them from their destructions" (Psalm 107:20).

"I shall not die, but live, and declare the works of the LORD" (Psalm 118:17).

"Heal me, O LORD, and I shall be healed; Save me, and I shall be saved, for You are my praise" (Jeremiah 17:14).

"For I am the LORD, I do not change; Therefore you are not consumed, O sons of Jacob" (Malachi 3:6).

"'But to you who fear My name The Sun of Righteousness shall arise with healing in His wings; and you shall go out and grow fat like stall-fed calves. You shall trample the wicked, for they shall be ashes under the soles of your feet on the day that I do this,' says the LORD of hosts" (Malachi 4:2–3).

"And even now the ax is laid to the root of the trees. Therefore every tree which does not bear good fruit is cut down and thrown into the fire" (Matthew 3:10).

PROPHETIC DECLARATION

"The Spirit of God has made me, and the breath of the Almighty gives me life" (Job 33:4). Therefore, O breath of the Almighty, breathe upon me that I may live to declare Your glory. I covenant my life to God Almighty for healing and good health.

Through the blood of Jesus, I overcome physical, moral and spiritual weaknesses. I declare that my physical, mental, and spiritual well-being is perfected in Jesus.

PRAYER POINTS

1. O blood of Jesus, plague every strongman behind any sickness, disease, and evil planting in my life, in Jesus' name.
2. It is written: "Behold, at that time I will deal with all who afflict you; I will save the lame, and gather those who were driven out; I will appoint them for praise and fame in every land where they were put to shame" (Zephaniah 3:19). Therefore, O blood of Jesus, undo my afflictions and set me free, in Jesus' name.

3. Any conscious and unconscious agreement with sicknesses and diseases in my life, I reject and renounce you by the blood of Jesus.

4. The raging horn of infirmities attacking my life, hear the Word of the Living God, it is written: "All the horns of the wicked also will I cut off; but the horns of the righteous shall be exalted" (Psalm 75:10). Therefore, I cut you off at the root, in the name of Jesus.

5. You evil plantation in my life, the Lord God, the Mighty Creator has a controversy against Thee, therefore, vanish from my life, in Jesus' name.

6. Through the blood of Jesus, I break free from generational infirmities, in Jesus' name.

7. It is written: "For the LORD your God is a consuming fire, a jealous God" (Deuteronomy 4:24). Therefore, thou consuming fire of the living God, flush out sickness and diseases from my life, in Jesus' name.

8. It is written: "And even now the ax is laid to the root of the trees. Therefore, every tree which does not bear good fruit is cut down and thrown into the fire" (Matthew 3:10). Therefore, Thou axe of God, uproot sickness and diseases out of my life, in Jesus' name.

9. Through the blood of Jesus, I reject every evil medical prophesy over my life in Jesus' name.

10. Blood of Jesus, flow into every part of my life and flush out every evil deposit, in Jesus' name.

11. I decree my body, soul, and spirit reject and eject evil plantation, in Jesus' name.

12. It is written: "But he was wounded for our transgressions, he was bruised for our iniquities: the chastisement of our peace was upon him; and with his stripes we are healed" (Isaiah 53:5). Therefore, I decree the wounds, the bruises, and the chastisement upon my

Lord Jesus Christ establish my healing now, in Jesus' name.

13. I decree that the angels of the living God excel in strength to minister perfect healing unto me now, in Jesus' name.

14. By the anointing of the Holy Spirit, I receive total deliverance from this yoke of infirmity, in Jesus' name.

15. By the power that created the heavens and the earth, I triumph over diseases and infirmities, in Jesus' name.

16. Any part of my life under the yoke of oppression and affliction, be set free now, in Jesus' name.

17. It is written: "But if I cast out demons with the finger of God, surely the kingdom of God has come upon you" (Luke 11:20). Therefore, by the finger of God, I cast out the demons attached to diseases and sickness in my life, in Jesus' name.

18. It is written: "Christ has redeemed us from the curse of the law, having become a curse for us (for it is written: 'Cursed is everyone who hangs on a tree'), that the blessing of Abraham might come upon the Gentiles in Christ Jesus, that we might receive the promise of the Spirit through faith" (Galatians 3:13–14). Therefore, every curse behind sickness and diseases in my life, in the name of Jesus Christ, break asunder.

19. O heavenly spare parts, be implanted into the malfunctioning parts of my body now, in Jesus' name.

20. By the blood of Jesus Christ, I decree life into every cell of my body, in Jesus' name.

21. I decree creative miracles and healing into my life, in Jesus' name.

22. Let God arise to perfect every good thing that concerns my health, in Jesus' name.

23. Holy Spirit, power of the highest, overwhelm me now, in Jesus' name.

24. Give thanks to God for manifestations of answered prayers, in Jesus' name.

Day Thirty
I SHALL NOT DIE
BUT LIVE!

Death is a torturer, a destroyer, a terminator, but it has been defeated by Him who has the keys of death and hell, my Lord Jesus Christ, the author of life. You can, without any doubt, be delivered from the bondage and fear of death and hell.

"I am He who lives, and was dead, and behold, I am alive forevermore. Amen. And I have the keys of Hades and of Death."

(Revelation 1:18)

Day Thirty
I SHALL NOT DIE BUT LIVE!

PRAISE AND WORSHIP
IT IS WRITTEN

B ut God will redeem my soul from the power of the grave, for He shall receive me" (Psalm 49:15).

"Let the groaning of the prisoner come before You; According to the greatness of Your power preserve those who are appointed to die" (Psalm 79:11).

"With long life I will satisfy him, and show him My salvation" (Psalm 91:16).

"I said, 'O my God, do not take me away in the midst of my days; Your years are throughout all generations'" (Psalm 102:24).

"For You have delivered my soul from death, my eyes from tears, and my feet from falling" (Psalm 116:8).

"I shall not die, but live, and declare the works of the LORD" (Psalm 118:17).

"I will ransom them from the power of the grave; I will redeem them from death. O Death, I will be your plagues! O Grave, I will be your destruction! Pity is hidden from My eyes" (Hosea 13:14).

"O Death, where is your sting? O Hades, where is your victory? The sting of death is sin, and the strength of sin is the law. But thanks be to God, who gives us the victory through our Lord Jesus Christ" (1 Corinthians 15:55–57).

"Who delivered us from so great a death, and does deliver us; in whom we trust that He will still deliver us" (2 Corinthians 1:10).

PROPHETIC DECLARATION

Jesus became flesh and blood that He might taste death and conquer death. He broke the shackle of death, and swallowed up death in victory. He rose again from death, as He spoilt principalities and powers. He is alive forevermore. This is the Lord that I serve and He lives in me forevermore.

PRAYER POINTS

1. Thanks be to God because, "Jesus Christ, the same yesterday, today and forevermore" (Hebrews 13:8).
2. It is written: "And your covenant with death shall be annulled, and your agreement with Sheol will not stand . . ." (Isaiah 28:18). Therefore, I reject and renounce the covenant between me and death.
3. In the name of Jesus, I break asunder covenants with death and hell.
4. Weapons of death and hell set against me shall not prosper, in Jesus' name.
5. In the name of Jesus Christ, I break loose from the union with dead relatives.
6. O Lord God of Host, shatter the attack of the gates of hell and death against my life, in Jesus' name.
7. In the name of Jesus, I reject sudden death.
8. Blood of Jesus, quench the sting of death in my life, in Jesus' name.

9. The pursuit of death and hell over my life, turn back and flee unto desolation, in Jesus' name.

10. Torture of death and hell, be drained out of my life by the fire of the Holy Spirit, in Jesus' name.

11. In the name of Jesus, I break loose from the fear of death, hell, and the grave.

12. You power of the coffin, I command your hold over my life to shatter by the fire of the Holy Spirit, in Jesus' name.

13. Every death ritual projected at me, fail and perish, in Jesus' name.

14. By the blood of Jesus, I overpower the summoning of death and hell, in Jesus' name.

15. In any way I've been marked for evil, blood of Jesus, annul it, in Jesus' name.

16. Thunder fire of God strike down the principalities of death, hell, and the grave set against my life, in Jesus' name.

17. Throne of death in my family line, be shattered asunder, in Jesus' name.

18. In the name of Jesus, I break free and break loose from the traps of death.

19. Angels of death and hell, lose your battles over my life, in Jesus' name

20. Blood of Jesus, seal up the gates of death and make it impossible for my soul to pass through, in Jesus' name.

21. Angels of life, win the battle on my behalf against the spirit of death and hell, in Jesus' name.

22. Resurrection life of my Lord Jesus Christ, perfect every good thing that concerns me, in Jesus' name.

23. Quickening power of the Holy Spirit, bring me alive, in Jesus' name.

24. Give thanks to God for answered prayers.

Day Thirty-One
OPEN DOORS

"Hear now what the LORD says: 'Arise, plead your case before the mountains, and let the hills hear your voice. Hear, O you mountains, the LORD's complaint, and you strong foundations of the earth; For the LORD has a complaint against His people, and He will contend with Israel.'"

(Micah 6:1–2)

Hindrances are moveable, obstacles are to be overcome, delays are not denials and opposition is to be triumphed over. Speak against closed doors and move forward.

Day Thirty-One

OPEN DOORS

PRAISE AND WORSHIP
IT IS WRITTEN

And you shall remember the LORD your God, for it is He who gives you power to get wealth, that He may establish His covenant which He swore to your fathers, as it is this day" (Deuteronomy 8:18).

"For You, O LORD, will bless the righteous; With favor You will surround him as with a shield" (Psalm 5:12).

"Blessed be the Lord, Who daily loads us with benefits, The God of our salvation!" (Psalm 68:19).

"The blessing of the LORD makes one rich, and He adds no sorrow with it" (Proverbs 10:22).

"The key of the house of David I will lay on his shoulder; So he shall open, and no one shall shut; and he shall shut, and no one shall open" (Isaiah 22:22).

"And I will give you the keys of the kingdom of heaven, and whatever you bind on earth will be bound in heaven, and whatever you loose on earth will be loosed in heaven" (Matthew 16:19).

"For assuredly, I say to you, whoever says to this mountain, 'Be removed and be cast into the sea,' and does not doubt in his heart, but believes that those things he says will be done, he will have whatever he says. Therefore I say to you, whatever things you ask when you pray, believe that you receive them, and you will have them" (Mark 11:23–24).

"For you know the grace of our Lord Jesus Christ, that though He was rich, yet for your sakes He became poor, that you through His poverty might become rich" (2 Corinthians 8:9).

"And to the angel of the church in Philadelphia write, 'These things says He who is holy, He who is true, He who has the key of David, He who opens and no one shuts, and shuts and no one opens'" (Revelation 3:7).

PROPHETIC DECLARATION

Blessed be the Lord Most High God, my Maker and my Everlasting Father, The All Sufficient, Eternal God, The Possessor of heaven and earth. He is my Fortress, my Deliverer, my Strength, my Shield, my High Tower and my exceedingly Great Reward.

The Lord my God is my Great Shepherd and has kept me as the apple of His eye. He has made me to ride on the high places of the earth, that I might eat the increase of the fields, and He made me to suck honey out of the rock, and oil out of the flinty rock.

PRAYER POINTS

1. It is written: "I have been young, and now am old, yet have I not seen the righteous forsaken, nor his seed begging bread" (Psalm 37:25). Therefore, according to the greatness of Your power, O God, deliver me from the grip of oppression, in Jesus' name.

2. With Your strong hand and with an outstretched arm, Almighty God, break asunder the strongman and the stronghold caging my destiny, in Jesus' name.

3. It is written: "The floods have lifted up, O LORD, the floods have lifted up their voice; the floods lift up their waves. The LORD on high is mightier than the noise of many waters, yea, than the mighty waves of the sea" (Psalm 93:3–4). Therefore, every flood lifted up to swallow my destiny, dry up now, in Jesus' name.

4. In the name of Jesus, I cast down every principality assigned against my open doors.

5. It is written: "Christ has redeemed us from the curse of the law, having become a curse for us for it is written: 'Cursed is everyone who hangs on a tree,' that the blessing of Abraham might come upon the Gentiles in Christ Jesus, that we might receive the promise of the Spirit through faith" (Galatians 3:13–14). Therefore, every curse attacking my open doors, break asunder now, in Jesus' name.

6. It is written: "casting down arguments and every high thing that exalts itself against the knowledge of God, bringing every thought into captivity to the obedience of Christ" (2 Corinthians 10:5). Therefore, I arrest every imagination and thought caging my joy and I render them desolate, in Jesus' name.

7. It is written: "The blessing of the LORD makes one rich, and He adds no sorrow with it" (Proverbs 10:22). Therefore, I receive blessings without sorrow, in Jesus' name.

8. My caged blessing, be un-caged and locate me now, in Jesus' name.

9. Stumbling blocks against my open doors, be rolled away now, in Jesus' name.

10. Every good thing that has been damaged in my life, be repaired by the blood of Jesus, in Jesus' name.

11. It is written: "The secret things belong unto the LORD our God: but those things which are revealed belong

unto us and to our children for ever, that we may do all the words of this law" (Deuteronomy 29:29 KJV). Therefore, O Lord God reveal deep secret of breaking forth into miraculous life onto me, in the name of Jesus.

12. My Almighty Father, stir up Your Throne and pour your blessings upon me, in Jesus' name.

13. Lord God, of Israel, arise and help me, in Jesus' name.

14. In the name of Jesus, I possess the keys of my destiny.

15. My diverted blessings, be restored unto me now, in Jesus' name.

16. It is written: "In his hand are the deep places of the earth: the strength of the hills is His also" (Psalm 95:4). Therefore, O Lord God, stir up the deep places of the earth to bless and favor my destiny, in Jesus' name.

17. It is written: "That He may set him with princes, even with the princes of His people" (Psalm 113:8). Therefore, I possess my open doors with joy, in Jesus' name.

18. I decree my horn be exalted with honor, in Jesus name.

19. I concentrate my open doors to wonderful testimonies, in Jesus' name.

20. It is written: "The steps of a good man are ordered by the LORD, and He delights in his way" (Psalm 37:23). Therefore, O Lord God, order my steps into outstanding miracles now, in Jesus' name.

21. Lord God, release your fresh breathe unto me to quicken my life unto miraculous exploits, in Jesus' name.

22. In the name of Jesus, let the angels of the living God bring good tidings unto me.

23. It is written: "And the glory of the LORD shall be revealed, and all flesh shall see it together: for the mouth of the LORD hath spoken it" (Isaiah 40:5). Therefore, O glory of the living God, manifest in my life now, in Jesus' name.

24. Give thanks to God for answered prayers.

PROPHETIC PRAYER FOR GREAT PROVISION AND FAVOR

God can yet favor you regardless of painful heart breaking and reproach.

"And Jabez called on the God of Israel saying, 'Oh, that You would bless me indeed, and enlarge my territory, that Your hand would be with me, and that You would keep me from evil, that I may not cause pain!' So God granted him what he requested."

(1 Chronicles 4:10)

Day Thirty-Two
PROPHETIC PRAYERS FOR GREAT PROVISION AND FAVOR

PRAISE AND WORSHIP
IT IS WRITTEN

For You, O LORD, will bless the righteous; With favor You will surround him as with a shield" (Psalm 5:12).

"The young lions lack and suffer hunger; But those who seek the LORD shall not lack any good thing" (Psalm 34:10).

"They are abundantly satisfied with the fullness of Your house, and You give them drink from the river of Your pleasures. For with You is the fountain of life; In Your light we see light" (Psalm 36:8–9).

"Blessed be the Lord, Who daily loads us with benefits, the God of our salvation!" (Psalm 68:19).

"For the LORD God is a sun and shield; The LORD will give grace and glory; No good thing will He withhold from those who walk uprightly" (Psalm 84:11).

"You will arise and have mercy on me; For the time to favor me, yes, the set time, has come" (Psalm 102:13).

"The blessing of the LORD makes one rich, and He adds no sorrow with it" (Proverbs 10:22).

"He who did not spare His own Son, but delivered Him up for us all, how shall He not with Him also freely give us all things?" (Romans 8:32).

"Blessed be the God and Father of our Lord Jesus Christ, who has blessed us with every spiritual blessing in the heavenly places in Christ" (Ephesians 1:3).

PROPHETIC DECLARATION

I'm precious in the sight of God; I'm honorable and loved by Him. God who created me for His glory has clothed me with favor.

I fearlessly and confidently draw strength from God's Shekinah presence. I, therefore, receive appropriate help and well-timed help for all my need, in Jesus' name.

Henceforth, I partake of God's great riches, knowing that my God shall supply all my needs according to His riches in glory by Christ Jesus.

PRAYER POINTS

1. Precious blood of Jesus, avail for me an endless provision now, in Jesus' name.
2. Thank you my Lord Jesus Christ, for plucking me out of the horrible pit and out of the miry clay, in Jesus' name.
3. Thank you my Lord Jesus Christ, for paying the price for my deliverance and that you alone are mighty to deliver me, in Jesus' name.
4. Thank you my Lord Jesus Christ, for delivering me from innumerable evils, in Jesus' name.
5. Thank you my Lord Jesus Christ, for delivering my life from shame, in Jesus' name.
6. Every cycle of shame, reproach and tragedy in my life, be shattered, in Jesus' name.

7. By the blood of Jesus, I reject, I renounce, and I denounce every inherited oppression in my life, in Jesus' name.

8. You spirit of the dunghill, I bind you and cast you out of my life, in Jesus' name.

9. You inherited spirit of debt, I curse you in the name of the Lord God of Host, I bind you and cast you out of my life, in Jesus' name.

10. You the powers of the pit, release me now and perish, in Jesus' name.

11. Every garment of ridicule and disfavor, I put you off now, in Jesus' name.

12. In the name of Jesus, I curse the root of hardship in my life, and I command it to perish now.

13. You spirit of wastage of divine resources, in my life, I put you under perpetual arrest, in Jesus' name.

14. My imprisoned glory, receive deliverance now and blossom, in Jesus' name.

15. I declare before the heavens and let the earth witness this declaration that my glory shall not sink, in Jesus' name.

16. All ye my profitable helpers arise, make haste to help me now, in Jesus' name.

17. The blood of Jesus is upon my life to attract great helpers to favor my life, in Jesus' name.

18. The helpers attached to my greatness in life, be released from your captivity and locate me now, in Jesus' name.

19. It is written: "Ah Lord GOD! Behold, thou hast made the heaven and the earth by thy great power and stretched out arm, and there is nothing too hard for thee" (Jeremiah 32:17 KJV). Therefore, O God of Abraham, Isaac and Jacob, arise and favor my life with exceeding joyful blessings, in Jesus' name.

20. It is written: "Behold, I am the LORD, the God of all flesh: is there any thing too hard for me?" (Jeremiah 32:27, KJV). Therefore, every good thing due to me, manifest now, in Jesus' name.

21. Angels of the Living God that excel in strength, clothe me with the garments of favor and glory, in Jesus' name.

22. O Lord God, open my eyes to behold my blessings and grant me the strength to possess them, in Jesus' name.

23. It is written: "I will instruct you and teach you in the way you should go; I will guide you with My eye" (Psalm 32:8). Therefore, I receive angelic escorts to my blessings, in Jesus' name.

24. Give thanks to God for answered prayers, in Jesus' name.

Day Thirty-Three
OVERWHELMING MERCIES

God's mercy is eternal and boundless. He's the "Father of mercies and the God of all comfort" (2 Corinthians 1:3). His mercies guarantee appropriate help and well-timed help.

Therefore, joyfully enter your season of mercies fearlessly and confidently.

Day Thirty-Three

OVERWHELMING MERCIES

PRAISE AND WORSHIP
IT IS WRITTEN

Then He said, "I will make all My goodness pass before you, and I will proclaim the name of the LORD before you. I will be gracious to whom I will be gracious, and I will have compassion on whom I will have compassion" (Exodus 33:19).

"Hear, O LORD, *when* I cry with my voice! Have mercy also upon me, and answer me" (Psalm 27:7).

"'Hear, O LORD, and have mercy on me; LORD, be my helper!' You have turned for me my mourning into dancing; You have put off my sackcloth and clothed me with gladness, To the end that *my* glory may sing praise to You and not be silent. O LORD my God, I will give thanks to You forever" (Psalm 30:10–12).

"Have mercy upon me, O God, According to Your loving-kindness; According to the multitude of Your tender mercies, Blot out my transgressions (Psalm 51:1).

"Show us Your mercy, LORD, And grant us Your salvation. (Psalm 85:7).

"Praise the LORD! Oh, give thanks to the LORD, for He is good! For His mercy endures forever" (Psalm 106:1).

"Help me, O LORD my God! Oh, save me according to Your mercy, That they may know that this is Your hand—That You, LORD, have done it!" (Psalm 109:26–27).

"Through the LORD's mercies we are not consumed, Because His compassions fail not. They are new every morning; Great is Your faithfulness" (Lamentations 3:22–23).

"Blessed *are* the merciful, For they shall obtain mercy (Matthew 5:7).

PROPHETIC DECLARATION:

". . . God be merciful to me a sinner" (Luke 18:13). My Lord and My God, the immutable one, He who was, and is and is to come, in Your self eternal existent power, manifest your greatness in my life, in Jesus' name.

PRAYER POINTS

1. Thanks be to God, who owns every beast of the forest and cattle upon a thousand hills, in Jesus' name.
2. Thanks be to God, who sits upon the circle of the earth, and the inhabitants are like grasshoppers, in Jesus' name (Isaiah 40:22).
3. Thanks be to God, who daily supplies all my needs according to His riches in glory by Christ Jesus (Philippians 4:19).
4. Thanks be to God and Father of my Lord Jesus Christ, who has blessed me with all spiritual blessings in heavenly places in Christ (Ephesians 1:3).
5. In Jesus' name, I declare before heaven that in Christ Jesus, I have obtained an inheritance, being predestined according to divine purpose.
6. Thanks be to God who works in me both to will and to do of His good pleasure (Philippians 2:13).

7. Thanks be to God, who bestows His love and tender mercies upon me.

8. Thanks be to God, who is able to keep me from falling, and to present me faultless before the presence of His glory with exceeding joy (Jude 24).

9. Thanks be to God, who spared not His own Son, but delivered Him up for us all (Romans 8:32).

10. Thanks be to God, who "is able to do exceedingly abundantly above all that we ask or think, according to the power that works in us" (Ephesians 3:20).

11. Jesus, my merciful and faithful High Priest, let the blood of Your atonement avail for me.

12. Jesus, "the Lion of the tribe of Judah, the Root of David" (Revelation 5:5), have mercy on me.

13. O Lord God, behold Your blood–sprinkled mercy seat and deliver me from iniquity, in Jesus' name.

14. In remembrance of your mercies, O Lord God of Israel, help me, in Jesus' name.

15. It is written: ". . . and mercy rejoices against judgment" (James 2:13), therefore, I triumph over every judgment against my life, in Jesus' name.

16. For your own name sake, O God of Israel, defend my life to save it, in Jesus' name.

17. It is written: "And her adversary also provoked her relentlessly, to make her fret" (1 Samuel 1:6), therefore, through the blood of Jesus, I overcome every relentless provocation to make me fret, in Jesus' name.

18. In the name of Jesus, I bind the spirit of error and cast it out of my life.

19. In the name of Jesus, I bind the spirit of disorderliness and cast it out of my life.

20. Through the blood of Jesus, I reject confusion and reproach, in Jesus' name.

21. Doors of mercies open unto me, now, in Jesus' name.

22. O Lord God, pour your mercies on me, in Jesus' name.
23. Henceforth, I rejoice in God's enduring mercies in Jesus' name.
24. Give thanks to God for answered prayers, in Jesus' name.

Day Thirty-Four
RECEIVING DIVINE GUIDANCE

God never leaves His own unguided. It is the will of God to guard your steps and decisions in the journey of life. He will certainly watch over and protect you.

This prayer section is for God to reveal His will concerning a certain situation of your life.

After this prayer section, be very specific of the area of your life you need guidance from God. As you lay it before the Lord, He would reveal His will and grant grace to obey.

"I will lift up my eyes to the hills—from whence comes my help?"

(Psalm 121:1)

Day Thirty-Four
RECEIVING DIVINE GUIDANCE

PRAISE AND WORSHIP
IT IS WRITTEN

The secret things belong to the LORD our God, but those things which are revealed belong to us and to our children forever, that we may do all the words of this law" (Deuteronomy 29:29).

"Show me Your ways, O LORD; Teach me Your paths. Lead me in Your truth and teach me, for You are the God of my salvation; On You I wait all the day" (Psalm 25:4–5).

"One thing I have desired of the LORD, that will I seek: That I may dwell in the house of the LORD all the days of my life, to behold the beauty of the LORD, and to inquire in His temple" (Psalm 27:4).

"The steps of a good man are ordered by the LORD, and He delights in his way" (Psalm 37:23).

"For the LORD Most High is awesome; He is a great King over all the earth. He will subdue the peoples under us, and the nations under our feet. He will choose our inheritance for us, the excellence of Jacob whom He loves" (Psalm 47:2–4).

"Every valley shall be exalted and every mountain and hill brought low; The crooked places shall be made straight and the rough places smooth; The glory of the LORD shall be revealed, and all flesh shall see it together; For the mouth of the LORD has spoken" (Isaiah 40:4–5).

"He reveals deep and secret things; He knows what is in the darkness, and light dwells with Him" (Daniel 2:22).

"For there is nothing covered that will not be revealed, nor hidden that will not be known" (Luke 12:2).

"And there is no creature hidden from His sight, but all things are naked and open to the eyes of Him to whom we must give account" (Hebrews 4:13).

PROPHETIC DECLARATION

Blessed be the LORD Most High God, possessor of heaven and earth—my shield and my exceedingly great reward. "Of a truth, God Almighty is the God of gods, and the Lord of kings, and a revealer of secrets" (Daniel 2:47 KJV). "For there is nothing covered that shall not be revealed; and hidden that shall not be known" (Matthew 10:26 KJV).

Therefore, O Lord God, according to Your Word, "I will instruct thee and teach thee in the way which thou shalt go, I will guide thee with mine eye" (Psalm 32:8 KJV). "Teach me Your way, O LORD, And lead me in a smooth path" (Psalm 27:11), in Jesus' name.

O God, revealer of secret things, reveal secret things regarding my life and lead me according to Your divine grace, that Your name alone may be glorified, in Jesus' name.

I shall walk and live habitually in the Holy Spirit. I shall be guided, controlled and responsive to the Holy Spirit, in Jesus' name.

PRAYER POINTS

1. It is written: "Having wiped out the handwriting of requirements that was against us, which was contrary to us. And He has taken it out of the way, having nailed

it to the cross" (Colossians 2:14). Therefore, blood of Jesus, cleanse, blot out, and nullify evil marks from my life, in Jesus' name.

2. It is written: "For God is not the author of confusion, but of peace" (1 Corinthians 14:33). Therefore, every cloud of confusion on my path, vanish now, in Jesus' name.

3. Any strongman assigned to bewitch the truth in my life, be smitten asunder, in Jesus' name.

4. Every curse of diversion and error, by the blood of Jesus, I destroy your grip over my life, in Jesus' name.

5. Any hold of the wicked on my life to attract evil into my life, wither now, in Jesus' name.

6. By the blood of Jesus, I blast asunder the trafficking of darkness assigned against my life, in Jesus' name.

7. Holy Spirit, inspire great dreams, visions and revelations to prosper my destiny, in Jesus' name.

8. O Lord God, let the eyes of my understanding be enlightened that I may know the secret behind this step (decision) I'm taking, in Jesus' name.

9. In the name of Jesus, I decree my spiritual senses be quickened by the power of the Holy Spirit.

10. It is written: "My sheep hear My voice, and I know them, and they follow Me" (John 10:27). My Lord Jesus, make me hear Your voice, and grant me the grace to follow, in Jesus' name.

11. By the blood of Jesus, I reject and refuse to listen to strange and uncertain voices, in Jesus' name.

12. Heavens, open unto me and let the angels of the living God ascend and descend for my sake, to guide my destiny to greatness, in Jesus' name.

13. Blood of Jesus, bless my dream life with divine ideas, in Jesus' name.

14. I covenant my sense organs to the Most High God by the blood of Jesus, to receive divine information, in Jesus' name.

15. In the name of Jesus, I put my thought life under the control of the Holy Spirit for divine inspiration.

16. In the name of Jesus, I decree into my life never to be subjected to errors, failure, or defeat.

17. The God of all possibilities, the all-knowing and all-powerful God Almighty, reveal Your greatness unto me, in Jesus' name.

18. Any veil separating me from the perfect will of God, be torn off now, in Jesus' name.

19. I arise into my divine heritage now, in Jesus' name.

20. Blockages in my inner man, be flushed out by the blood of Jesus, in Jesus' name

21. O Lord God, bless me with eyes that see, and ears that hear, in Jesus' name.

22. May my thoughts and imagination be filled with divine revelations, in Jesus' name.

23. Holy Spirit, guide and comfort me with divine revelations, in Jesus' name.

24. Give thanks to God for answered prayers.

Day Thirty-Five
THIRSTING FOR GOD'S PRESENCE

It is time to desire and pant after God. In this prophetic miracle journey, deepen your love for God's presence. Commit yourself to the things of eternal values. Your destiny is secured in knowing more about God.

"You will show me the path of life; In Your presence is fullness of joy; At Your right hand are pleasures forevermore."

(Psalm 16:11)

Day Thirty-Five
THIRSTING FOR GOD'S PRESENCE

PRAISE AND WORSHIP
IT IS WRITTEN

"My soul thirsts for God, for the living God. When shall I come and appear before God?" (Psalm 42:2).

"O God, You are my God; Early will I seek You; My soul thirsts for You; My flesh longs for You In a dry and thirsty land Where there is no water. So I have looked for You in the sanctuary, To see Your power and Your glory. Because Your loving-kindness is better than life, My lips shall praise You. Thus I will bless You while I live; I will lift up my hands in Your name" (Psalm 63:1–4).

"I spread out my hands to You; My soul longs for You like a thirsty land" (Psalm 143:6).

"The hope of the righteous will be gladness, but the expectation of the wicked will perish" (Proverbs 10:28).

"For surely there is a hereafter, and your hope will not be cut off" (Proverbs 23:18).

"So shall the knowledge of wisdom be to your soul; If you have found it, there is a prospect, and your hope will not be cut off" (Proverbs 24:14).

"But whoever drinks of the water that I shall give him will never thirst. But the water that I shall give him will become in him a fountain of water springing up into everlasting life" (John 4:14).

"And Jesus said to them, 'I am the bread of life. He who comes to Me shall never hunger, and he who believes in Me shall never thirst'" (John 6:35).

"They shall neither hunger anymore nor thirst anymore; the sun shall not strike them, nor any heat; for the Lamb who is in the midst of the throne will shepherd them and lead them to living fountains of waters. And God will wipe away every tear from their eyes" (Revelation 7:16–17).

PROPHETIC DECLARATION

O Lord my God, I am earnestly waiting for Your presence. I am expectant, longing sincerely for Your revealing majesty. Manifest Your glory now in me, in Jesus' name.

I enthrone Jesus and the fullness of His power in my life. I cease from pursing unprofitable things, but choose to chase after righteousness in the Holy Spirit, in Jesus' name.

PRAYER POINTS

1. Blood of Jesus, purge my senses now, in Jesus' name.
2. Every veil on my eyes, be consumed by the Holy Spirit fire, in Jesus' name.
3. Holy Spirit fire, consume every clouded vision affecting my life, in Jesus' name.
4. Holy Spirit, quicken me out of the valley into glorious heights, in Jesus' name.
5. Every wall or partition between me and God's presence, break asunder, in Jesus' name.
6. In my eternal walk with God, I shall neither be weary nor faint, in Jesus' name.

7. Every strange fire kindled in my life be consumed by the Holy Spirit fire, in Jesus' name.

8. Every diversion in my search for God, be annulled by the blood of Jesus.

9. I cast the slumbering spirit out of my life, in Jesus' name.

10. I cast the lustful spirit out of my life, in Jesus' name.

11. I cast the lukewarm spirit out of my life, in Jesus' name.

12. I paralyze the works of the flesh in my life, in Jesus' name.

13. My spirit man, be un-caged, in Jesus' name.

14. Rivers of living water, flood the dryness of my life, in Jesus' name.

15. My spirit, be delivered from the power of the oppressors, in Jesus' name.

16. Blood of Jesus, heal my wounded spirit, in Jesus' name.

17. Holy Spirit, create a sincere love and compassion of God into my life, in Jesus' name.

18. I decree to my life to bring forth glorious fruits, in Jesus' name.

19. I receive grace to seek after God, His righteousness and kingdom, in Jesus' name.

20. O Lord God, visit me now with your glorious presence, in Jesus' name.

21. Profitable helpers, be attracted to me now, in Jesus' name.

22. Glorious signs and wonders, manifest now in my life, in Jesus' name.

23. O Lord God, satisfy my thirst and my search for you with your divine presence, in Jesus' name.

24. Give thanks to God for answered prayers.

Day Thirty-Six
IGNITING THE POWER OF THE HOLY SPIRIT

Let your spirit man catch the fire of the Holy Spirit.
Ignite the fire and explode in the Holy Spirit.

"To the one we are the aroma of death leading to death,
and to the other the aroma of life leading to life. And
who is sufficient for these things?"

(2 Corinthians 2:16)

Day Thirty-Six

IGNITING THE POWER OF THE HOLY SPIRIT

PRAISE AND WORSHIP
IT IS WRITTEN

The earth was without form, and void; and darkness was on the face of the deep. And the Spirit of God was hovering over the face of the waters. Then God said, 'Let there be light'; and there was light" (Genesis 1:2–3).

"Create in me a clean heart, O God, and renew a steadfast spirit within me. Do not cast me away from Your presence, and do not take Your Holy Spirit from me. Restore to me the joy of Your salvation, and uphold me by Your generous Spirit" (Psalm 51:10–12).

"But truly I am full of power by the Spirit of the LORD, and of justice and might, To declare to Jacob his transgression and to Israel his sin" (Micah 3:8).

"And the angel answered and said to her, The Holy Spirit will come upon you, and the power of the Highest will overshadow you; therefore, also, that Holy One who is to be born will be called the Son of God" (Luke 1:35).

"He who believes in Me, as the Scripture has said, out of his heart will flow rivers of living water" (John 7:38).

"But you shall receive power when the Holy Spirit has come upon you; and you shall be witnesses to Me in Jerusalem, and in all Judea and Samaria, and to the end of the earth" (Acts 1:8).

"But if the Spirit of Him who raised Jesus from the dead dwells in you, He who raised Christ from the dead will also give life to your mortal bodies through His Spirit who dwells in you" (Romans 8:11).

"But as it is written: Eye has not seen, nor ear heard, nor have entered into the heart of man the things which God has prepared for those who love Him. But God has revealed them to us through His Spirit. For the Spirit searches all things, yes, the deep things of God" (1 Corinthians 2:9–10).

"Now the Lord is the Spirit; and where the Spirit of the Lord is, there is liberty. But we all, with unveiled face, beholding as in a mirror the glory of the Lord, are being transformed into the same image from glory to glory, just as by the Spirit of the Lord" (2 Corinthians 3:17–18).

PROPHETIC DECLARATION

Give ear, O ye heavens, and I will speak; and hear, O earth, the words of my mouth. My Words shall drop as the rain, my speech shall carry live and divine presence. I will proclaim the name of the LORD of host; I will ascribe greatness unto the Most High God. He is my Rock. His work is perfect, I am His handiwork, for I am fearfully and wonderfully made. "The Spirit of God has made me, and the breath of the Almighty gives me life" (Job 33:4).

Therefore, by the quickening of the Holy Spirit, I speak as the oracle of God. For, the words that I speak are spirit and they are life. According to Your Word, O God, "And it shall come to pass afterward, that I will pour out my Spirit upon all flesh" (Joel 2:28 KJV). Therefore, O Lord God, pour out your Holy Spirit upon me now, in Jesus' name.

PRAYER POINTS

1. Any power, spirit, or personality drawing energy from the heavenlies to block my open heaven, be scattered, in Jesus' name.

2. Any power, spirit or personality drawing energy from the sun, the moon and the star to attack my destiny, be scattered, in Jesus' name.

3. Every projection of weariness and confusion into my life, become an empty waste, in Jesus' name.

4. Every interference in the supernatural to cage my spirit, be scattered and be destroyed, in Jesus' name.

5. You principalities assigned to hinder God's presence in my life, I cast you down, in Jesus' name.

6. It is written: "The Lord our God is a consuming fire" (Hebrews 12:29). Therefore, thou consuming fire of the living God, consume every captivity in my life, in Jesus' name.

7. Any evil dedication hindering the manifestation of the Holy Spirit in my life, be abolished by the blood of Jesus, in Jesus' name.

8. Every conscious and unconscious covenant and evil dedication hindering the manifestation of the Holy Spirit in my life, break asunder now, in Jesus' name.

9. Holy Spirit, arrest my inner man and purge it with your fire, in Jesus' name.

10. Every defilement in my body, soul and spirit, be purged by the Holy Spirit fire, in Jesus' name.

11. Holy Spirit, as you brooded, hovered and moved over the deep, in the beginning, manifest yourself in my life, in Jesus' name.

12. Thou Spirit of the LORD, that raised Jesus from the dead, quicken and deliver me from every bondage, in Jesus' name.

13. I have not received the spirit of bondage, therefore, I bind the spirit of bondage in my life and command freedom into my life, in Jesus' name.

14. Thou Holy Spirit Who helps our infirmities, release your strength in me and help me, in Jesus' name.

15. Thou Holy Spirit Who searches the heart and knows the mind, unfold the will of God unto me, in Jesus' name.

16. [Lay your right hand on your belly] Thou rivers of living water, flow through my life, in Jesus' name.

17. "When the enemy shall come in like a flood, the Spirit of the LORD shall lift up a standard against him" (Isaiah 59:19). Therefore, Holy Spirit, lift up a standard against my enemies and put them to flight, in Jesus' name.

18. My spirit man, ignite the fire of God's presence now, in Jesus' name.

19. Holy Spirit, strengthen me with might in my inner man, in Jesus' name.

20. The seal of redemption by the Holy Spirit is upon me, therefore, I command every evil mark upon my life be blotted out, in Jesus' name.

21. The hour has come and now is, Holy Spirit fill my life with divine glory, in Jesus' name.

22. My life, manifest the divine gifts now, in Jesus' name.

23. Henceforth, I shall manifest the wonders and the glory of God, in Jesus' name.

24. Give thanks to God for answered prayers.

Day Thirty-Seven
QUENCH NOT THE SPIRIT

Now that you are set on fire for God, let your spirit be aroused, get excited in the Holy Spirit and press on for great things. Get involved in the kingdom work and slack not.

"Let not your hands be slack."

(Zephaniah 3:16, KJV)

Day Thirty-Seven
QUENCH NOT THE SPIRIT

PRAISE AND WORSHIP
IT IS WRITTEN

Then I said, 'I will not make mention of Him, nor speak anymore in His name.' But His word was in my heart like a burning fire shut up in my bones; I was weary of holding it back, And I could not" (Jeremiah 20:9).

"I will give you a new heart and put a new spirit within you; I will take the heart of stone out of your flesh and give you a heart of flesh. I will put My Spirit within you and cause you to walk in My statutes, and you will keep My judgments and do them" (Ezekiel 36:26–27).

"The wind blows where it wishes, and you hear the sound of it, but cannot tell where it comes from and where it goes. So is everyone who is born of the Spirit" (John 3:8).

"It is the Spirit who gives life; the flesh profits nothing. The words that I speak to you are spirit, and they are life" (John 6:63).

"For I am not ashamed of the gospel of Christ for it is the power of God to salvation for everyone who believes, for the Jew first and also for the Greek" (Romans 1:16).

"For you did not receive the spirit of bondage again to fear, but you received the Spirit of adoption by whom we cry out, 'Abba, Father.' The Spirit Himself bears witness with our spirit that we are children of God" (Romans 8:15–16).

"But as it is written: Eye has not seen, nor ear heard, nor have entered into the heart of man the things which God has prepared for those who love Him. But God has revealed them to us through His Spirit. For the Spirit searches all things, yes, the deep things of God" (1 Corinthians 2:9–10).

"Do not quench the Spirit" (1 Thessalonians 5:19)

"Therefore I remind you to stir up the gift of God which is in you through the laying on of my hands. For God has not given us a spirit of fear, but of power and of love and of a sound mind" (2 Timothy 1:6–7).

PROPHETIC DECLARATION

I am hungry and thirsty for your divine presence, fill me, O God. I lift the vessel of my life before your throne; pour Your grace and mercy upon me.

"Create in me a clean heart, O God, and renew a steadfast spirit within me" (Psalm 51:10).

PRAYER POINTS

1. O God, forgive me for despising and limiting Your greatness, in Jesus' name.
2. I repent before the Lord, of my sin of lukewarmness and backsliding, in Jesus' name.
3. I receive the forgiveness of the Holy Spirit for not honoring His presence, in Jesus' name.
4. O Lord God, restore unto me the joy of Your presence, in Jesus' name.
5. I bind and I cast out the spirit of slumber in my life, in Jesus' name.
6. Let the mandate of darkness over my life, fail, in Jesus' name.

7. The stronghold of temptation that draws me to sin, be shattered in Jesus' name.

8. Throne of iniquity over my life, be scattered, in Jesus' name.

9. The networking of darkness over my life, be scattered, in Jesus' name.

10. Blood of Jesus, seal up leakages in the vessel of my life, in Jesus' name.

11. Blood of Jesus, purge the vessel of my life from impurity, in Jesus' name.

12. As the Lord lives and as His Spirit lives, the light of my glory shall not be quenched, in Jesus' name.

13. The wall or partition between me and God, collapse now, in Jesus' name.

14. In the name of Jesus, my glory shall not sink.

15. Every exchange of my birthright be restored unto me, in Jesus' name.

16. My love for God and His kingdom that has been diverted, be restored now, in Jesus' name.

17. Weariness projected to my soul, depart now, in Jesus' name.

18. In the name of Jesus, I break loose from the yoke of discouragement.

19. Holy Spirit, heal my wounded spirit, in Jesus' name.

20. Holy Spirit, break forth into my life to liberate me from confusion of soul, in Jesus' name.

21. My glory that I've traded with the world, be restored now, in Jesus' name.

22. Anointing of the Holy Spirit, break forth into my life, in Jesus' name.

23. My zeal and my love for God and His kingdom, be rekindled, in Jesus' name.

24. Give thanks to God for answered prayers.

Day *Thirty-Eight*
FULFILLING PROPHETIC DESTINY

God has ordained you to achieve completion of miracles. Set into performance and enjoy manifold miracles.

"Be strong and of good courage, and do it; do not fear nor be dismayed, for the LORD God—my God—will be with you. He will not leave you nor forsake you, until you have finished all the work for the service of the house of the LORD."

(1 Chronicles 28:20)

Day Thirty-Eight
FULFILLING PROPHETIC DESTINY

PRAISE AND WORSHIP
IT IS WRITTEN

So God heard their groaning, and God remembered His covenant with Abraham, with Isaac, and with Jacob. And God looked upon the children of Israel, and God acknowledged them" (Exodus 2:24–25).

"He who planted the ear, shall He not hear? He who formed the eye, shall He not see? He who instructs the nations, shall He not correct, He who teaches man knowledge?" (Psalm 94:9–10).

"You will arise and have mercy on Zion; For the time to favor her, yes, the set time, has come" (Psalm 102:13).

"He permitted no one to do them wrong; Yes, He rebuked kings for their sakes, Saying, 'Do not touch My anointed ones, and do My prophets no harm'" (Psalm 105:14–15).

"When you pass through the waters, I will be with you; And through the rivers, they shall not overflow you. When you walk through the fire, you shall not be burned, nor shall the flame scorch you" (Isaiah 43:2).

"Before I formed you in the womb I knew you; Before you were born I sanctified you; I ordained you a prophet to the nations" (Jeremiah 1:5).

"Then you shall know that I am in the midst of Israel: I am the LORD your God and there is no other. My people shall never be put to shame" (Joel 2:27).

"Being confident of this very thing, that He who has begun a good work in you will complete it until the day of Jesus Christ" (Philippians 1:6).

"He who calls you is faithful, who also will do it" (1 Thessalonians 5:24).

PROPHETIC DECLARATION

As the Lord Jehovah lives and as His Spirit lives, the determinate counsel of God for my life shall not be aborted, but shall be fulfilled, in Jesus' name.

My divine destiny is secured in Jesus because my life is hid with Christ in God. I shall without doubt possess my promised land of glory, in Jesus' name.

PRAYER POINTS

1. Thanks be to God for his calling and election over my life, in Jesus' name.
2. Thanks be to God for his unfailing grace and love for me, in Jesus' name.
3. Thanks be to God, who has formed me, and known me, and destined me for greatness from my mother's womb.
4. I consecrate my journey in life to my Lord Jesus Christ and the power of His blood.
5. Blockages in my inner man be cleared by the blood of Jesus.
6. Every unprofitable journey of my life, be withdrawn and be cleansed by the blood of Jesus.
7. Any decision stirring up captivity in my life, be abolished by the blood of Jesus.

8. My destiny shall not be trapped in the wilderness of life, in Jesus' name.

9. You spirit of un-accomplishment, vanish from my life, in Jesus' name.

10. The yoke of impossibility to achieve good things in my life, be shattered, in Jesus' name.

11. Spirit of profitless hard working, flee from my life, in Jesus' name.

12. O Lord God, restore my glorious visions, in Jesus' name.

13. The vehicle of my destiny, advance and prosper, in Jesus' name.

14. You Spirit of barrenness, flee from my life, in Jesus' name.

15. Evil manipulation over my destiny, be abolished by the blood of Jesus.

16. My crown of honor and dignity, be restored, in Jesus' name.

17. O Lord God, restore my reasoning unto me, in Jesus' name.

18. O God that changes times and seasons, change my times and seasons for good, in Jesus' name.

19. My glorious prophetic destiny, be restored now, in Jesus' name.

20. My life, break free from multiple traps and bondages, in Jesus' name.

21. O Lord my God, You have the master plan of my life; guide me into it, in Jesus' name.

22. O Lord my God, reveal Your plans for my life, in Jesus' name.

23. My Lord Jesus, the Author and Finisher of my faith, strengthen me to fulfill my prophetic destiny now, in Jesus' name.

24. Give thanks to God for answered prayers.

Day Thirty-Nine
ARISE AND SHINE

Let your heart rejoice exceedingly for your life is eternally transformed.

"Show me a sign for good, that those who hate me may see it and be ashamed, because You, LORD, have helped me and comforted me."

(Psalm 86:17)

Day Thirty-Nine
ARISE AND SHINE

PRAISE AND WORSHIP
IT IS WRITTEN

For the LORD of hosts has purposed, and who will annul it? His hand is stretched out, and who will turn it back?" (Isaiah 14:27).

"The Spirit of the Lord GOD is upon Me, because the LORD has anointed Me to preach good tidings to the poor; He has sent Me to heal the brokenhearted, to proclaim liberty to the captives, and the opening of the prison to those who are bound; to proclaim the acceptable year of the LORD, and the day of vengeance of our God; to comfort all who mourn, to console those who mourn in Zion, to give them beauty for ashes, the oil of joy for mourning, the garment of praise for the spirit of heaviness; That they may be called trees of righteousness, the planting of the LORD, that He may be glorified" (Isaiah 61:1–3).

"You are My battle-ax and weapons of war: For with you I will break the nation in pieces; With you I will destroy kingdoms; With you I will break in pieces the horse and its rider; With you I will break in pieces the chariot and its rider; With you also I will break in pieces man and woman; With you I will break in pieces old and young; With you I will break in pieces the young man and the maiden; With you also I will break in pieces the shepherd and his flock; With you I will break in pieces the farmer and his yoke of oxen; And with you I will break in pieces governors and rulers" (Jeremiah 51:20–23).

"Also He said to me, 'Prophesy to the breath, prophesy, son of man, and say to the breath, "Thus says the Lord GOD: Come from the four winds, O breath, and breathe on these slain, that they may live."' So I prophesied as He commanded me, and breath came into them, and they lived, and stood upon their feet, an exceedingly great army" (Ezekiel 37:9–10).

"So I will restore to you the years that the swarming locust has eaten, the crawling locust, the consuming locust, and the chewing locust, My great army which I sent among you. You shall eat in plenty and be satisfied, and praise the name of the LORD your God, Who has dealt wondrously with you; and My people shall never be put to shame. Then you shall know that I am in the midst of Israel. I am the LORD your God and there is no other. My people shall never be put to shame" (Joel 2:25–27).

"But on Mount Zion there shall be deliverance, and there shall be holiness; The house of Jacob shall possess their possessions" (Obadiah 1:17).

"And they glorified God in me" (Galatians 1:24).

"That the God of our Lord Jesus Christ, the Father of glory, may give to you the spirit of wisdom and revelation in the knowledge of Him, the eyes of your understanding being enlightened; that you may know what is the hope of His calling, what are the riches of the glory of His inheritance in the saints, and what is the exceeding greatness of His power toward us who believe, according to the working of His mighty power which He worked in Christ when He raised Him from the dead and seated Him at His right hand in the heavenly places, far above all principality and power and might and dominion, and every name that is named, not only in this age but also in that which is to come. And He put all things under His feet, and gave Him to be head over all things to the church, which is His body, the fullness of Him who fills all in all" (Ephesians 1:17–23).

"For you died, and your life is hidden with Christ in God" (Colossians 3:3).

PROPHETIC DECLARATION

I proclaim Jesus Christ is my power, determining the course of events of my life. My future is secured, my past is renewed in the Holy Spirit and my present is delivered from evil. I am destined to prosper. Therefore I decree to my life, in Jesus' name, "Arise, shine; For your light has come! And the glory of the LORD is risen upon you" (Isaiah 60:1).

PRAYER POINTS

1. Thanks be to God because the rods of them that smote me are broken asunder, in Jesus' name.
2. Thanks be to God for His glorious counsel shall be established in my life, in Jesus' name.
3. It is written: "For I know the thoughts that I think toward you, says the LORD, thoughts of peace and not of evil, to give you a future and a hope" (Jeremiah 29:11). Therefore, I decree that my future will align with God's glorious plan, in Jesus' name.
4. It is written: "There are many plans in a man's heart, nevertheless the LORD's counsel—that will stand" (Proverbs 19:21). Therefore, the purposes and plans of God for my life, come to pass, in Jesus' name.
5. Holy Spirit, fortify my life with your signs and wonders, in Jesus' name.
6. Angels of the living God, shield my life against evil attacks, in Jesus' name.

7. Blood of Jesus, re-enforce your glorious presence in my life, in Jesus' name.

8. I decree to my life never to respond to evil summoning, in Jesus' name.

9. Rivers of the living water, flow into my life to refresh my soul, in Jesus' name.

10. It is written: "He permitted no one to do them wrong; Yes, He rebuked kings for their sakes" (Psalm 105:14). Therefore, O Lord God, forbid powers, spirits and personalities from oppressing me, in Jesus' name.

11. It is written: "Through God we will do valiantly, for it is He who shall tread down our enemies" (Psalm 108:13). Henceforth, with God's help, I shall do mighty things, in Jesus' name.

12. It is written: "The LORD has broken the staff of the wicked, the scepter of the rulers;" (Isaiah 14:5). Therefore, the staff and the scepter of the wicked against my life, be broken, in Jesus' name.

13. Thus says the Lord God of Host to the oppressors of my soul, "How you are fallen from heaven . . . How you are cut down to the ground" (Isaiah 14:12), in Jesus' name.

14. O ye fiery, flying serpents lifted up against my life, be slain by the sword of the Lord God of Host, in Jesus' name.

15. Through the blood of Jesus, I withdraw the vehicle of my destiny from stagnancy and backwardness, in Jesus' name.

16. O the angels of the living God, strike the heavens and the earth and silence the voices of my oppressors, in Jesus' name.

17. It is written: "While the earth remains, seedtime and harvest, cold and heat, winter and summer, and day and night shall not cease" (Genesis 8:22). Therefore, I

call forth the seasons of the earth to prosper and favor me, in Jesus' name.

18. It is written: "For exaltation comes neither from the east nor from the west nor from the south. But God is the Judge: He puts down one, and exalts another" (Psalm 75:6-7). Therefore, O Lord God, gloriously promote my destiny, in Jesus' name.

19. O rushing mighty wind of the Holy Spirit, re-enforce divine presence into my life, in Jesus' name.

20. O angels of the living God, sound the greatness of God Almighty in my life unto all the earth, in Jesus' name.

21. The joy of my heart shall not cease and I shall dance for victory, in Jesus' name.

22. O Lord God Jehovah, crown my destiny with glorious success, Jesus' name.

23. It is written: "Ask a sign for yourself from the LORD your God; ask it either in the depth or in the height above" (Isaiah 7:11). Therefore, O Lord God, I ask for signs and wonders to overwhelm my life, in Jesus' name.

24. Thank God for answered prayers, in Jesus' name.

Day Forty
PRAISE WARFARE

"Let everything that has breath praise the LORD!"
(Psalm 150:6)

Triumph in praise because you have just completed your prophetic journey to miracles. Look around you and behold the miracles. Celebrate the miracles and share your testimonies.

Day Forty
PRAISE WARFARE

"Great and marvelous are your deeds, Lord God Almighty; just and true are your ways, King of the ages" (Revelation 15:3, NIV).

"Who shall not fear You, O Lord, and glorify Your name? For You alone are holy. For all nations shall come and worship before You, For Your judgments have been manifested" (Revelation 15:4).

"You are worthy, O Lord, to receive glory and honor and power; For You created all things, And by Your will they exist and were created" (Revelation 4:11).

I join the innumerable company of angels to say, "'Worthy is the Lamb!' saying with a loud voice: 'Worthy is the Lamb who was slain to receive power and riches and wisdom, and strength and honor and glory and blessing!' And every creature which is in heaven and on the earth and under the earth and such as are in the sea, and all that are in them, I heard saying: 'Blessing and honor and glory and power Be to Him who sits on the throne, and to the Lamb, forever and ever!'" (Revelation 5:12–13).

"And crying out with a loud voice, saying, 'Salvation belongs to our God who sits on the throne, and to the Lamb!' All the angels stood around the throne and the elders and the four living creatures, and fell on their faces before the throne and worshiped God, saying: 'Amen! Blessing and glory and wisdom, thanksgiving and honor and power and might, be to our God forever and ever. Amen'" (Revelation 7:10–12).

"Saying: We give You thanks, O Lord God Almighty, the One who is and who was and who is to come, because You have taken Your great power and reigned" (Revelation 11:17).

Let my voice be like the sound of many waters saying, Hallelujah! "And I heard, as it were, the voice of a great multitude, as the sound of many waters and as the sound of mighty thunderings, saying, Alleluia! For the Lord God Omnipotent reigns!" (Revelation 19:6).

"After these things I heard a loud voice of a great multitude in heaven, saying, Alleluia! Salvation and glory and honor and power belong to the Lord our God!" (Revelation 19:1).

"I will extol You, O LORD, for You have lifted me up, and have not let my foes rejoice over me. O LORD my God, I cried out to You, and You healed me. O LORD, You brought my soul up from the grave; You have kept me alive, that I should not go down to the pit. . . . You have turned for me my mourning into dancing; You have put off my sackcloth and clothed me with gladness, to the end that my glory may sing praise to You and not be silent. O LORD my God, I will give thanks to You forever" (Psalm 30:1–3, 11–12). I praise You, O God, for Your name alone is excellent, and Your glory is above the earth and heaven.

"O Lord, open my lips, And my mouth shall show forth Your praise" (Psalm 51:15). Awake my soul and magnify Jehovah, the Lord Most High God, the Lord of kings, the revealer of secrets, my Almighty Father. I give unto the Lord God glory due unto His Holy name. I exalt Him in the beauty of His holiness. I am exceedingly glad and I rejoice in Your mercies because You have made Your face to shine upon me.

Blessed be the Lord, for He has shown me His marvelous kindness in the land of the living. How excellent is Your loving kindness O God, for You alone deserve my praises and adoration.

O heavens and the earth, and everything therein, unite with me to praise the Lord Most High, the Holy One of Israel. Thanks be to God for His unsearchable greatness. Thanks be to God for He upholds all that fall and raises up all those who bow down.

Thank You, my Lord Jesus, for forgiving me all my sins.

Thank You, my Lord Jesus, for satisfying my longing soul, and filling my hungry soul with goodness.

Thank You, my Lord Jesus, for redeeming my soul from sins, sicknesses, destruction, and death.

Thank You, my Lord Jesus, for saving my life from sudden destruction.

Thank You, my Lord Jesus, for not allowing the grave to eat me up.

Thank You, my Lord Jesus, for rescuing my life from the pit of darkness.

Thank You, my Lord Jesus, for not allowing troubles to swallow me up.

Thank You, my Lord Jesus, for causing me to drink of the river of Your pleasure.

Thank You, my Lord Jesus, because You delight in my wellbeing.

Thank You, my Lord Jesus, for preserving and keeping my soul from evil.

Thank You, my Lord Jesus, for quieting the storms and tempests roaring at me.

Thank You, my Lord Jesus, for not delivering me unto the will of my enemies.

Thank You, my Lord Jesus, for subduing my enemies under me.

Thank You, my Lord Jesus, for the precious gift of eternal life.

Thank You, my Lord Jesus, for enduing me with the Holy Spirit to comfort and guide me.

Thank You, my Lord Jesus, for being my helper.

Thank You, my Lord Jesus, because You've blessed me indeed.

About the Author

Pastor David O. Komolafe is the founding Pastor of Above All Christian Gathering, a fast-growing, full-gospel ministry, with its headquarters in Toronto, Canada.

He holds a Masters in Practical Ministry from Wagner Leadership Institute, Colorado Springs, United States of America. He has been used by God for the past three decades in Church planting and prophetic intercession in Africa, Israel, Europe, United States and Canada.

He is married to a prophetic intercessor—Mercy—and he is blessed with three prophetic children—Esther, Grace and Shalom.

To order additional copies of this title call:
1-877-421-READ (7323)
or please visit our web site at
www.winepressbooks.com

If you enjoyed this quality custom published book,
drop by our web site for more books and information.

www.winepressgroup.com
"Your partner in custom publishing."

And also visit our web site at
www.davidkomolafe.com
and
contact him at his e-mail address:
author@davidkomolafe.com